THE DIARY

OF A

JESUS

TAG-ALONG

By Carol Asher

The Diary of a Jesus Tag-Along

Copyright © 2023 by Carol Asher

ISBN 13: 979-8-9885146-0-2
Library of Congress PCN 2023917038

To contact Carol Asher or to order a copy of this book,
please visit www.amitypublications.com

Design and Layout by
AMITY Publications

Printed in the United States of America

"Come, follow me," Jesus said.
(Matthew 4:19)

"Seek first the kingdom of God and
God's righteousness.
And all [other] things will be given
to you as well."
(Matthew 6:33)

"Ask and it will be given to you;
seek and you will find;
knock and the door will be opened to you.
For all those who ask receive;
those who seek find;
and to those who knock,
the door will be opened."
(Matthew 7:7-8)

AUTHOR'S NOTES

The seed of this diary came from a question from several younger friends who are peripherally attached to different churches. They asked for help to make sense of all this Lenten "stuff" and how to better understand a fuller meaning of Lent (like ashes and giving something up) and Holy Week and Good Friday and Easter... and what should be their "correct" response to all that.

As I thought about it more... "making sense" is a cerebral exercise... thinking everything out in some orderly fashion (that's what we study in theology). On the other hand, things of faith are internal, emotional, spiritual and... quite frankly, often messy. Faith doesn't "make sense". Faith is heart and guts. Faith is personal. If faith links with the cerebral at all, it's endeavoring to find the words and expressions to verbalize those "things of faith". Alas, the words many times fall short in the midst of divine experiences.

Perhaps because of my personality type, I usually try to insert myself into the scriptural story in order to feel the issue more fully, hoping that will lead me to a better understanding. So, here I am imagining that it is the year 33 and I am living somewhere in the Galilee region. I have met the itinerant teacher in person whom I have heard about for quite a while... and I have decided to become one of the followers of Jesus. And I'd like to share this experience as if I were writing a diary.

Although most of the events described here are scriptural, there are many other things that are figments of the imagination of this diarist. As I shared these reflections, I had some questions about the liberties taken in the writing: ("Did that REALLY happen? I've never heard that story before."). Since the diarist would have had no access or knowledge beyond the Hebrew Scriptures at the time of this writing, there are no specific mentions of New Testament citations, although the disciples frequently shared what they remembered of their experiences with Jesus. To make it easier for readers less familiar with scripture, I have added endnotes with citations to steer the reader to explore the biblical texts. There are also notes to further explain some references in the writing. These citations and notes are indicated by superscripts in the writing; they are listed in the endnotes under the numbered entry of the diary.

Let me explain one "word" you will see very often: G*d. Learned Jews would NEVER write the Hebrew name for God. Ancient prohibitions against writing it protected that treasured name from being erased. At times, the initials "YHWH" would be written, but when that particular verse was read out loud, the name "Yahweh" would NOT be pronounced, because it was too precious… the reader would substitute "hashem" (meaning "the name"). This lesson was instilled into all those being educated. The diarist explains that she learned to read and write Hebrew along with her brothers… and she would certainly have obeyed this practice. It is included here in the English to remind readers of the exceptional nature of our G*d… even as it refers to G*d's name.

Suggestions

This is not meant to be a book that is read from start to finish. Rather, it begins a couple of days before what we call "Palm Sunday" and offers one entry per day during those tumultuous several weeks. Then, after the Resurrection, the reflections stretch out through Pentecost (seven weeks later) and the aftermath of that celebration. There are indications of the subjects and timeline in the list that follows. I urge you to read through and reflect on only one entry at a time; take some time as you accompany this diarist on this journey.

So, welcome to this diary of a "Jesus tag-along". I invite you to become another "tag-along" and imagine yourself right there in each entry. What would you have thought and felt? How would you have reacted if you were there? What questions would you have wanted to ask Jesus (or, maybe, the other followers) if you had the chance? What would it have taken for you to continue on this journey? What would you have noted in your own diary? There are some suggestions along the way to STOP and REFLECT.

I pray you completely enjoy the experience of this "journey".

Shalom/Salaam
Carol

TIMELINE

Entry/Page

1. On a Wednesday evening... my beginning

Dear Diary,

Here I am. I begin this diary as I embark on this adventure. My name is Carol Asher. I am proud and humbled to claim the name "Asher" (from one of the twelve tribes, meaning "blessed" and "fortunate") along with my given first name because I really feel blessed at this time.

I guess I am now what might be called a "Jesus tag-along". In our group, there are twelve men whom Jesus specifically called to follow him.[1,2] I think they have been together for about three years now. It really is an unlikely grouping... and I'm not sure how or why Jesus has asked this interesting and diverse group to stick with him as close as he has.

Anyway... there are quite a few of us who travel along with that core group. Even though we aren't "the chosen" as they are, it's a real privilege to eavesdrop on the conversations that Jesus has with them. It seems that after a full day of walking, touching the many needy people who approach the group, and teaching all along the way, Jesus almost always settles in around the fire each night to listen to the many questions and then to try to explain some of the lessons he gave as we were all walking.

As a woman, I feel good that I can help the group by gathering and preparing food for everyone. We are traveling so much that we don't carry a lot with us. Along with some cooking utensils, I thought to bring some thread and a needle to assist those helpless men when it comes to taking care of the rips and tears in their clothing. I like the way that Jesus smiles his thanks to us... just for being there.

I am also privileged to know how to read and write. It's pretty unusual for a girl to learn, but as long as I had finished my chores, my parents never minded when my brothers shared their knowledge with me after they returned from their daily classes.

I love my family; they were a little curious when I told them about the new teacher who had come into our town with his strange entourage... but their curiosity turned to anger when I told them that I felt somehow "pulled" to follow the group. My father bellowed: "This idea of yours makes NO SENSE!" I couldn't find the words to explain... it wasn't about "making sense" to my mind... the invitation to follow them tugs at my heart, wanting to FEEL MORE fully. The call to join the group makes my feet and hands want to engage this new experience more completely. My family tried so hard... but they could not stop me.

So, here I am... a "Jesus tag-along".

It has occurred to me that I should write down some of the things that are happening as we travel, as well as some of tidbits of conversation that we hear. These are merely the thoughts of a simple woman... but perhaps, someday, they will be important in telling the story of this special teacher. Although I have no idea what is in store for Jesus and the rest of us, I sense deep down that there is something incredible about Jesus and what he is teaching us.

2. Thursday... traveling into Jericho

Dear Diary,

    I haven't been with this group for very long, but even I noticed that Jesus seemed a little "off" today for some reason... not at all like his normal, caring and outgoing nature. His impatience almost came to the surface when we arrived near the outer gates of the city of Jericho. There was a blind man there;[1] it seems he was a "regular" beggar at the gate, for all the townspeople knew him by name. As we passed by the spot, the blind man must have heard something about Jesus. Those near to him were trying to hold him back and quiet him down, but he suddenly yelled out "Jesus, Son of David, have mercy on me!" I wonder HOW he has heard about our teacher... and even more, WHAT he has heard about him.

    Jesus stopped as the man approached. There was a strange sound in Jesus' voice as he off-handedly questioned, "What do you want me to do for you?" Of course, the blind man wanted nothing more than have his sight restored. Jesus had a vague look on his face as if the request were as simple as breathing. He waved his hand in the air and simply declared that the man's sight would be restored, since his faith had made him well. Such a miracle... and Jesus acted like it were simply child's play!

    Initially, there was the most profound silence at Jesus' words. When the people saw Bartimaeus (that's the blind man's name) run off marveling at all the ordinary things he was seeing for the very first time... the impact of the event sank into people's minds and hearts. Almost immediately, the street started filling with people marveling at the blind man's sudden and total recovery. This is the first time that I am witness to one of Jesus' healing miracles that I've heard about... I am utterly amazed and awed by the power Jesus has at his fingertips (literally!) and a little confused at his calm nonchalance.

We hadn't gone far into Jericho, when Jesus looked up into a tree along the way and saw a man who had climbed up there to be above the crowd.[2] Jesus stopped... and the crowd silenced. Jesus called to the man "Zaccheus, come on down here!" I wonder how Jesus knows the names of strangers. As the short little man came down and stood in the street, Jesus told him that he was going to his house to stay for the evening. There was a murmur in the crowd; I caught the words "tax collector" and "too rich for his own good". It was obvious that the crowd didn't like this Zaccheus guy and were surprised that the teacher would invite himself to spend time at his house instead of spending time in a fine home of one of Jericho's more prominent residents.

The last we saw of Jesus, he had his arm wrapped around Zaccheus' shoulder, assuring him that he would be saved with all the other sons of Abraham. Jesus looked so happy as he and Zaccheus made their way through the crowd.

I thought I was beginning to understand what Jesus was about... but I realize that I REALLY don't understand anything at all!

Jesus is not with us as we gather around the fire tonight after the evening meal. As we recline, there is much whispering and very little laughter.

Perhaps he is still with Zaccheus. But, after the events of this day... maybe Jesus has gone off alone instead of lingering around the warmth of the fire, as is his custom. I'm not sure when Jesus ever sleeps, for, many times, as the rest of us settle into our capes to sleep, he walks off alone to find a quiet place away from the group. There are times during the night when I wake up and see him still out there... talking to himself and praying. But always, in the morning, he seems refreshed. I guess we will find out about his whereabouts as a new day dawns.

SOMETHING is happening here, and I can't put my finger on the feelings in the pit of my stomach.

3. Late Friday afternoon... beginning of the Sabbath

Dear Diary,

We have stopped early today as we all prepare for the sundown beginning of Sabbath.[1,2] Our meager meal was served to all with unusual quiet; for some reason, there was little of the casual chatter that characterizes this unusual "family" gathering.

The way Jesus has been talking with everyone is somewhat unsettling. He seems so much more earnest as he speaks. Today there were no stories about farmers or fishermen... no, today the hushed, yet intense tones of his lessons seemed so much more ominous and serious. Jesus spoke about prayer, and about entrance into "the kingdom", and about salvation, and about gratitude, and about service... and he even spoke about his own death. I do NOT want to hear that!

There was so much that I didn't quite understand... and as I looked around at the faces of the chosen disciples, I realized that they, too, had many more questions. Tonight, Jesus just kept speaking, not stopping as he is accustomed to give examples and to invite questions. I think Jesus is somewhat impatient with his students; I think he knows that they don't "get it".

I have a gut feeling that something is about to change for us all.

I must stop now, for dear Hannah, who is the oldest woman in our midst, is serving as mother and has begun to light the candles to call us into the spirit of Sabbath.

4. Saturday Evening... after the Sabbath has ended

Dear Diary,

This has been such a strange day! Because of Sabbath restrictions, we couldn't travel very far. It is dark now and I can again pick up writing materials, for our day of rest has ended. For once, all of us, including the women in the group, are treated as guests, rather than preparing the meal for everyone.

We have passed this Sabbath day in Bethany. Those in our group have come here often to relax, bathed in the grand hospitality of the siblings, Mary and Martha and Lazarus.[1] They are Jesus' dear friends; he embraces them as if they were HIS own family.

I had not yet become a "tag-along" when a while ago, Jesus had been summoned by the sisters because Lazarus was very ill.[2] I heard that those sisters were quite disturbed, because Jesus had tarried on the road and didn't arrive here in Bethany until after Lazarus had died and had laid in the tomb for several days. When Jesus finally arrived, he evidently tried to convince the sisters that Lazarus wasn't really dead... and with tears in his eyes, he ordered people to roll the stone away from the front of Lazarus' grave and ordered Lazarus to come out. I get shivers just hearing the disciples tell that story! I can't imagine this idea of coming back to life, but Jesus told those who gathered around that HE was the RESURRECTION and the LIFE for all those who would believe in him. Of course, that story was retold on this night as we gathered for a meal... and many words of gratitude and amazement were raised to the Almighty. This is the first time that I hear the word "resurrection" used like this... and I wonder what it could possibly mean for us... and for me personally. Then, we were in for a surprise. Mary usually stayed back and helped in the cooking area, as

Martha bustled around all the guests to make sure all the prepared food was served properly.[3] Mary had been lingering with us instead of helping Martha, listening to all that was said, especially from Jesus. It was a surprise when MARY... of all people... approached the group with a large alabaster jar of nard. Its costly oil is sometimes used, in small amounts, to anoint a cherished guest who has entered a home. As she uncorked the jar, the strong aroma of that perfume rose in the room.[4,5] But... then... Mary suddenly BROKE the WHOLE jar open, pouring its entire contents over Jesus' head!! After a moment of stunned silence, some in our group began to criticize Mary's wasteful act, saying that the jar could have been sold for a lot of money that could have been given to the poor who really needed it. Initially, I guess everyone thought that Mary wanted to add that aroma to the telling of the story of raising Lazarus from the dead, for nard is one of the perfumed oils that is sometimes used to wrap the body of a loved one at burial. But we are all left to wonder WHY she would spill the entire jar of that oil, even though she dearly loved Jesus. Jesus praised the gift; he seemed to understand her actions, although the rest of us were truly perplexed as what this all meant.

Because Judas kept all the money for our group, he certainly knew how much that oil was worth. He seemed so incensed by the extravagant pouring out of all that oil... and the fact Jesus condoned that waste... that he abruptly stood up and left the house. He's so upset; I wonder if someone should go and follow him... (hmm... I smile to myself when I reread the double meaning of the word "incensed". Judas was incensed after Jesus was incensed. As we end this Sabbath day, I wish I could feel pleased at my own choice of words.)

In spite of being guests in the home of dear friends, I doubt that many of us will sleep well tonight

5. Evening of the first day of the week... going into Jerusalem

Dear Diary,

There are rumors flying all over the city that the religious leaders are conspiring to hurt our leader and teacher Jesus, especially after that business with the blind man the other day. I don't understand it! I pray that they are only rumors, but I am afraid they aren't.

Jesus has been insistent that he wants to be in Jerusalem for the Passover feast this year. He seems to disregard the rumors that are swirling all around us.

Today... as we said our good-byes to Mary, Martha and Lazarus and left Bethany, we had barely arrived at the top of the hill, called the Mount of Olives, to catch a glimpse of Jerusalem stretched out before us, when Jesus stopped us. I was hoping that he was rethinking the whole idea of going across the valley and up into the grand city. But that wasn't his idea at all!

He told two of the disciples to go into the nearby village and get a young donkey that he somehow knew would be tied up outside a house there.[1] Jesus gave them the specific instructions to tell the owner, if questioned... that "the Lord had need of the animal". WHAT in the world did Jesus have in mind for a DONKEY??

When the disciples returned, they put their cloaks on the back of the little animal and Jesus sat right on it. We saw that donkey shift a little with the unaccustomed weight on its back, but it did not balk at all. Our teacher and master sat right up there, as if he were riding a magnificent white stallion!

Immediately, many of the disciples and the other "tag-alongs" threw their outer garments onto the road to cut down the dust... an action usually offered to a grand royal visitor.[2] They broke palm branches from the trees along the way and waved them, singing praises to G*d and saying, "Blessed is the King who comes in the name of the Lord! Peace in heaven and glory in the highest!" I remember, years ago, my father teaching us to proclaim those verses, as our family walked up into city of Jerusalem, because that was the custom as pilgrims made their way into the city. But this time... it was almost like people were cheering right AT Jesus as he passed by!

People... strangers that we have never seen... started coming out of their homes and joining in with loud voices! I heard one old man exclaim that he was seeing the fulfillment of an Old Testament prophecy[3] about the children of Jerusalem rejoicing, for they would see their king and savior coming to them, humbled and riding on a donkey. All of a sudden, my heart swelled... and my eyes saw this man, this Jesus whom I have loved and "tagged along after" in a new and glorious light! I tremble even as I write these words!

The road down the side of the Mount of Olives is very steep and narrow. As more and more people joined the procession, it was harder and harder for Jesus to pass through, riding proudly on that donkey.

Most people pressed to the side of the road to allow Jesus to pass. But in the shouting throng, there were some Temple leaders who stood with their arms crossed and refused to let Jesus move forward.[4] They demanded that he silence the shouts of the gathered crowd. Instead of quieting the people, Jesus calmly told the leaders that the stones in the path would shout out, even if the human voices were silenced. I have NEVER heard stones shout, but I'm beginning to believe that Jesus could even make that happen!

We pushed forward little by little. When we had reached the last little hill on the road... the great walls of Jerusalem loomed high and solid before us. We were still a ways off, but our Holy City seemed so close to us. All of a sudden, the noise stopped. We looked around and then looked at Jesus... and saw tears running down his face.[5] He was near sobbing as he seemed to talk right to the city, saying something about the things that make for peace that are now hidden from view... and that the huge walls now protecting the city would one day encircle the inhabitants like a prison. His tears and his words filled my heart with dread... a feeling that quickly darkened my joyful feelings of just moments before.

As quickly as the glorious procession had started... it was over. The shouting and the palm-waving stopped... and people retreated back into their homes.

It didn't seem possible that we had been on this pathway almost all day. With no more fanfare, Jesus slid off the little donkey and led most of us through the wide gates of the city and right into the temple area. Jesus barely looked around and immediately turned around... and we began to recross the valley and head back to Bethany. Our stomachs rumbled with hunger... and our hearts trembled with a feeling of gloom. The jubilation of the morning's praises was darkened with an uneasy dread.

When this first started, I thought today's was a triumphal parade[6]; I thought that maybe people had some special inkling, some keen insight to recognize something about Jesus that even the disciples and we "tag-alongs" don't quite realize. At the same instant that I want to see Jesus in a much larger picture, as I reflect on this morning's ride into Jerusalem, there is a fear growing in my being that... (oohh... I don't even like writing this!) makes today feel more like the doomed procession of a convicted prisoner.

I honestly don't know what to think or feel. What can ANY of us think and feel?

6. Monday... Going again to Jerusalem and into the Temple

Dear Diary,

I'm not sure I can write at this point; I'm shaking so much that ink is blotching the paper without recording my thoughts. In all the time that I have been with this group, I have never seen Jesus in such a mood, if I can even call it a "mood".

Today was a continuation of the earnestness of last evening. Jesus spoke with such intensity! He repeated some of the things he has said in the last several days... about masters and slaves... about the salvation of all people... about the challenges of believing... about the future of "the nation"... and again, he spoke about his own death. The more Jesus tries to teach, the less I can really understand. All the individual words that I hear are understandable enough, but when I put them all together, the meaning behind the words is far beyond my comprehension. I wonder if we will ever make sense of all this.

We set out from Bethany again this morning and headed down the same steep, narrow path into Jerusalem as yesterday. There was no donkey... no palms waving... no jubilant cries of "Hosanna!" The dust blew into our faces because no cloaks were spread on the pathway. Our group was hushed as we zig-zagged our way down to cross the valley. The sun was already high in the sky and I assume everyone was getting as thirsty as I was.

Jesus spotted a little fig tree off the side of the road that was flowering.[1] He went up to it hoping to gather some fruit to eat. As he approached the lone tree, he stopped short and seemed to be angry at the fig tree. He actually CURSED that poor little tree for having leaves and no fruit! No sooner had the words come out of his mouth... that little tree withered and died! We stood there in dread and amazement... and then Jesus turned to us and told us that IF we had faith and didn't doubt... that we too would be able to do similar things... that we could even tell a whole mountain to move... and that MOUNTAIN WOULD MOVE ITSELF INTO THE SEA. Jesus accentuated each word as he looked us in the eye: "whatever... you... ask... in... prayer... believing... you... will... receive." I can hardly breathe, even as I try to remember those words to write them down.

Barely had those words dug into our hearts when Jesus abruptly turned to continue the walk into Jerusalem. He doesn't WALK now... he STRIDES! It's like there's no time to waste getting from here to there (wherever THERE is). I can barely keep up.

He led us right into the Temple area. I thought, as usual, that Jesus and the men would continue through the first courtyard to the inner place where Jesus has regularly stood and taught all those who gathered there. As a woman, I'm not allowed to follow them in there, so I depend on the other disciples to share some of what Jesus had said.[2]

All around the edges of the huge outer court where everyone can enter (even the Gentiles) are many tables and tents set up to sell the perfect animals to be offered for sacrifice.[3] There are other booths where men exchange foreign money into the proper shekels to pay the Temple tax to the priests. Since we are entering into the Passover season, there are many more visitors and much more business for those merchants.

Today, Jesus went no further than that outer court... and... he absolutely exploded as he overturned the tables and pulled down the fencings and awnings around the animals who became terrified and scattered. The money-changers looked on in horror as Jesus grabbed their money boxes and emptied them out in the courtyard.[4]

I have never seen such pandemonium... even on the days when thousands of people flocked to the Temple in times of holy obligation. Jesus' words echoed above all the rest of the noise... they were not the normal, regulated tones of his teachings, but rather loud, angry words proclaiming G*d's scriptural truths that "the house of the Lord will be called a house of prayer for all nations." For the second time in the same day, he cursed! This time the recipients were the merchants; Jesus charged them with transforming the Temple into a den of robbers.

My heart was stuck in my throat to see the destruction in that courtyard... and then to see the looks on the faces of the Temple leaders who came out from the sacred inner court to see what all the noise was about. Even if they agreed with the notion that the Temple was G*d's house of prayer, they must have been incensed with the damage all around them. Obviously, it would cut into the payments they would receive for their leadership during these holy days... they simply could not allow the likes of Jesus to interrupt their "sacred" schedules.

Jesus also saw their faces and their stance. Rather than being afraid, Jesus challenged those leaders even more... he defiantly told them that this "minor damage" in the courtyard was nothing compared to the total destruction of the entire Temple that was to come.

Then Jesus looked around at the many blind and lame people who had come into that outer court hoping for some pity in the form of alms from those pilgrims coming to Jerusalem for the festival. Jesus called them out to approach him... and he healed every single one of them. I could hardly breathe, for I remember my father telling us the old stories of King David's victory over the Jesubites to establish Jerusalem as capital for the Hebrews.[5] Now, we watched Jesus mock a thousand years of religious tradition as those healed passed into the courtyard of the women... and knowing that the men would be allowed right into the inner courts.

Up to now, there was probably nothing they could charge Jesus with... but I fear that Jesus has gone too far this time. I pray that all this will somehow settle down and that Jesus and the rest of our group can go back to teaching and healing. I don't understand exactly where that point is... but I fear that Jesus has gone past the point of no return. I'm afraid for him... and for the rest of us.

STOP AND REFLECT

Imagine this setting... all that turmoil amid "normal Temple business". Look carefully at Jesus... who is often portrayed as "meek and mild", but here He is modeling "holy anger". What tables were toppled over? Could one of them have been YOUR own table?

7. Tuesday... facing the Pharisees

Dear Diary,

Oh, how I wish I could write much faster, so I could record all that Jesus said today! I'm hoping that each of us will remember some parts of all this clearly, so that we can reconstruct all these lessons sometime soon. Even as we talked all this over among ourselves this evening, there are some things remembered... and quickly, others in the group protest, claiming that Jesus didn't say that, or had worded it differently. I fear that, although these teachings seem very important now, we won't remember them well enough when the time comes...[1]

We again went with Jesus down over the Mount of Olives and into the Temple. When we entered the outer courts, the Temple leaders were more visible than they have in the past. Maybe it's because of the coming Passover feast... but they quickly surrounded Jesus and started to pepper him with questions and accusations like never before.

They asked him point blank who in the world he thought he was... speaking as he did about matters of faith and salvation.[2] Unlike yesterday, Jesus kept his cool and countered every question. Instead of being on the defensive, Jesus asked the Temple leaders probing questions. If it weren't so serious, it would have been comical, because at times, those religious leaders had to withdraw and talk among themselves as to the "proper" answer before they could go back and deliver it to Jesus.

It seemed like they were trying to trap Jesus into saying something that would be blasphemous or heretical... but Jesus kept turning the tables on their questions by making them go deeper and deeper into their own understanding of the ancient scriptures. When they got to a point of any particular question where they realized that they were digging themselves into a hole, they changed the subject.

They asked about Jewish history and the future of our Jewish nation. For the first time in days, Jesus told a story to illustrate his answer. But instead of being the informative story about a man who owned a vineyard that I had heard before... this one ended in the murder of the owner and the total destruction of the vineyard.[3] The religious leaders only narrowed their eyes as they tried to digest that answer.

But they didn't give up. They continued to pepper Jesus with questions about taxes, and the idea of resurrection, and about G*d's great commandment. When all was said and done, those leaders had to admit that Jesus had answered every single question well. They certainly seemed more frustrated than angry.

Those priests and scribes finally retreated and left Jesus to teach the people gathered around. I was surprised that Jesus didn't lead the men into the inner court to teach as he had many times in the past; he stayed where even we women were allowed to gather and listen. Could it be that what Jesus is talking about is for ALL OF US?? Not just the men, but the women and children as well?

There is so MUCH to think about... to wonder about... to pray about. At least, for the moment, the religious leaders seem to have reluctantly accepted Jesus and all that he is teaching. I really hope that their retreat will mark the end of the hostile feelings the Temple authorities have against him.

We all look forward to celebrating the Passover together. Jesus has been adamant about observing this special time here in Jerusalem. Maybe with the lessening of anger, Jesus will be safe, as will the rest of us.

8. Wednesday... more teachings for the disciples

Dear Diary,

Today has been a quiet day. We are all so tired... not so much from physical activity, but we are strangely mentally and emotionally exhausted. As much as I appreciate this day of reduced activity, it's... it's... an uneasy rest. So much has happened, just in the last week or so.

We didn't venture out anywhere... it probably isn't safe for Jesus to show his face in the city. Lately as we've traveled, Jesus has had a different look in his eyes... I can't quite find an adequate word... it's like looking far ahead at a different goal. More often than not, he passes right by the children, or by a lame person begging at the side of the road, or by a group of women carrying heavy loads... he doesn't stop to bless, to heal, to teach, to encourage, as if he doesn't have time for such menial tasks. This isn't his normal practice, and this confuses me.

Today even Jesus was more subdued. In these last several days, he has been speaking... almost pleading... as he sits with us and explains his ideas.[1,2] There's been an edge to his voice, and he doesn't use stories to illustrate those high ideas. There's a lot that I don't quite understand, but as Jesus speaks, he looks deep into our faces... and maybe even further into our hearts, as if he's willing us... no! even compelling us to comprehend what he means. As I look around at the faces of his chosen disciples, I see them constantly eyeing each other... almost as if they are checking if their companions understand better what Jesus is saying. It gives me shivers when he speaks about his own death, as if this vibrant young teacher will die before his time. He assures us that it will not be the end, but that there's something extraordinary planned for the future. I cannot imagine life without him leading this special group of people.

Jesus' mother and several family members have arrived from Nazareth to spend Passover with him and us. It's nice that his family will be here for the festivities, as well as his gathered family of disciples and tag-alongs. Jesus drapes his arm around his mother's shoulders... but he seems a little distant, like he is feeling the need to be (I don't know) more grown-up, perhaps, and beyond the role of being Mary's adult son.

The Passover[3] is just hours away now. I so look forward to this annual commemoration of the liberation of G*d's people. There is more noise everywhere as more and more people journey into Jerusalem, as is the custom. I had never been able to make this pilgrimage with my family. I supposed that I would be thrilled when I finally got to celebrate in the holy city, but for some reason, the atmosphere doesn't feel exciting. I don't know what to think, except that I believe, deep down, that THIS Passover will be unlike any other one that we have ever celebrated before.

Judas has been away all day. I suppose that he is arranging for us to gather for the Passover.[4] With so many visitors in the city, it might be difficult to find a large enough place, but Judas has a way of getting what he wants and needs.

STOP AND REFLECT

All the followers were anticipating the celebration of the age-old Passover for some sense of familiar. What rituals or commemorations do YOU look forward to? What makes them special? Do they comfort? Do they energize?

---

9. Thursday late night... first night of Passover

Dear Diary,

A while ago, I couldn't keep my eyes open, and now I can't sleep. I can barely hold my quill, but I think I should write while I have the chance. I don't want to forget all these important things... yet I don't want to remember my despair.

There was a flurry of activity today to get everything ready for the Passover Feast. We women were busy preparing the meal and procuring all the special elements that are needed for the Passover ritual, even though we hadn't yet heard where we would gather. That question was on the minds of the disciples, so they asked Jesus where he would like us to go to make all things ready for the feast. We had assumed that Judas left to arrange all that, so I was a little confused, when, during the late morning, Jesus told Simon Peter and John to go into the holy city and follow a man they'd meet who was carrying a pitcher of water.[1] I was startled! I know every woman would be very busy preparing food and arranging all the necessary items... but to ask a MAN to fetch water was almost laughable. The disciples hesitated for only an instant... from past experience, they knew that Jesus had the whole scenario in mind. So they went out; a short time later, they sent word that all had been arranged just as Jesus had predicted.

We all went to the home of a family in the holy city; it was an enormous room, though very simple... on the second story of their home in a rather quiet neighborhood away from the Temple area. Those two disciples had seen to it that the several tables were properly set up. The twelve chosen disciples reclined with Jesus around one long table and the rest of us "tag-alongs" gathered around other tables at the other side of the room. We women took turns to serve all that we had prepared.

The host family had made their own preparations in

their downstairs living area. As everyone began to sit down, the young daughter of the owner came in with the usual sign of hospitality; she carried a basin of water and towel to wash the feet of guests invited into their home. Contrary to custom, Jesus himself took the towel and basin![2] I couldn't imagine what to think! Everyone was stunned... but Peter found his voice and objected to Jesus washing his feet. Jesus insisted, saying that Peter and the others must allow this lowly task that Jesus had taken on. He talked about masters and servants... and that neither is greater than the other. Jesus spoke rather forcefully when he commanded that we love one another and in the sense of serving each other, we must wash each other's feet. Everyone knows that once the dust of traveling has been washed from the feet of travelers, then they are clean... but when Jesus finished washing everyone's feet, he said in a strange voice that not all of us had been cleansed. I really didn't understand that because I looked around and saw that Jesus had not missed anyone.

It was so comforting to hear the familiar passages of the Passover story... recalling how G*d delivered our Hebrew ancestors from the clutches of Egyptian slavery. "Why is this night different from all the others?" was the ritual question. After all the topsy-turvy lessons, it was so good to hear the age-old questions and answers... and to be assured that G*d had a plan for G*d's people from the beginning. I wonder what message Moses would bring us today as we struggle with the Roman oppression... is there still a plan for liberation?

With all the familiar rituals that make this feast of unleavened bread so special, there was a nice relaxed feeling in that room. That is... until... Jesus took a large piece of the flat bread and started passing it around; as he did, he looked at the faces of his friends and said that one of them would betray him.[3] I wondered if I had heard him correctly. Betray... him?? Surely, not one of those chosen followers! Could it be one of the "tag-alongs" at our other tables? But no! He was looking only at those at his own table. Each disciple questioned and then vehemently denied any such prospect... Just as Jesus spoke that it would be better if that one had never been born... he passed the bread to Judas and told him to go quickly to do what was to be done. Judas abruptly got up and left... while we puzzled at what Jesus was commanding Judas to do. Surely, the one trusted with all the money of this group would not turn on Jesus.

Again, Jesus returned to the Passover ritual... and the tense feelings in the room dissipated only a little bit. Toward the end, Jesus lifted the last cup of wine[4]... traditionally called the Elijah cup, which was meant as G*d's assurance of the plan for a messiah to come and restore G*d's people. Jesus took a deep breath and put the cup down and picked up a piece of flat bread. He broke it into pieces and passed it around the table, saying that the broken bread was his body broken and given for each of them. When he picked up the cup again, he departed from the traditional words once again... and he referred to the wine as his own blood poured out in a brand-new covenant. He invited all present to drink it, remembering him as the giver of the cup. The profound silence that followed spoke volumes! I know we are supposed to remember this very moment, but I cannot begin to tell you how or even why.

I'm not sure how the squabble started, perhaps the disciples were trying to make sense of what Jesus was saying. Peter boasted something about understanding it all better than the others... and Jesus quickly rebuked him and told Peter to hold fast to his faith. Peter straightened his shoulders and told Jesus that nothing could shake him or his faith... that he (Peter) was ready and willing to always follow Jesus, even to death. Jesus sighed and shook his head, before quietly telling Peter that before the cock crowed in the new morning that Peter would deny even knowing Jesus, not once, but three times.[5] We watched as Peter wilted at this portent. WHAT did Jesus know about what was going to happen? First Judas... then Peter... would Jesus have some prediction about each of us? I shiver to think WHAT Jesus knows about me...

Soon after, Jesus stood up to leave the room. He headed out across the valley into the Garden of Gethsemane.[6] This was a favorite place for Jesus to relax with us all. Peter was the last one to follow out of the room; it was like he was in a trance; he finally shook himself aware and hurried to catch up with the rest of the group. It was very late by the time we arrived. As we all settled into the coolness of that quiet garden, Jesus asked us to remain vigilant as he went off at a distance to pray. We watched him... it was obvious that he was troubled and that this particular time of prayer was not refreshing as his prayer time usually was. I tried... I really tried to keep my eyes open... but the gentle breathing of the disciples and other companions was like a lullaby. I was drifting to sleep when I heard Jesus' voice, calling us to be awake and WATCH. This time, he took John and James... and Peter... with him as he went a little further into the garden and fell to the ground in agonizing prayer. Again, I tried... and so did the others; even John and James and Peter slipped into sleep. Just as I felt my heavy eyelids close, I remembered his words that one of us would betray him. As much as I wanted to watch with him, my chest sighed with the knowledge that I, too, was guilty of betrayal in some form.

All of a sudden, the quiet garden was filled with noise.[7] By the light of dozens of torches, we saw soldiers wielding swords and clubs, and the chief priests and a bunch of scribes and elders... and, oh my gosh, Judas was leading them all! He went right up to Jesus and kissed him. WHAT could that mean? In the chaos, swords were raised; Peter took up a sword and in a fit of anger took a wild swing, cutting off the ear of a servant of the high priest. The noise immediately stopped when Jesus loudly shouted for everyone to be quiet. Jesus touched the servant's ear to heal it... and then turned to the soldiers and priests. In the midst of this danger, he taunted them, asking if they realized that he could ask his Father to send a legion of angels to protect him. My heart wanted to shout: "Ask, dear Jesus, ask! Ask for that protection!" It was obvious that the angry mob was intent on arresting our Jesus and taking him away! WHY didn't he ask for those angels to keep this all from happening?!? I couldn't believe it when he gave in, saying that was what needed to happen for the prophecies of Scripture to be fulfilled! But, Jesus, what about all those stories about the Kingdom of G*d being a future kingdom of PEACE and LIFE??

The mob took Jesus away with them... down the hill and across the valley. I don't know where they have taken him. It was both Roman soldiers and Hebrew religious authorities who arrested him... WHAT are they arresting him for? And WHO is "in charge"? I am SO ashamed of myself and my companions; in fear and without Jesus, we just scattered. I know that we should have stayed together... I walked around in a daze for a little while, but I didn't see any of the disciples and met up with only a few of the other "tag-alongs". For the moment, some of us are sheltered in the back room of some acquaintance here in Jerusalem.

I try to recall the ritual words for protection. I wish I could remember the words when Jesus taught us how to pray! I have a feeling that Jesus could use all the prayers we can muster. For that matter, I think each of us needs all the prayers we can manage.

Oh, Almighty G*d... show me the way... ANY WAY! Now I believe that Jesus really is your son! Protect him! Ohhhh, my Lord!!

10. Friday evening... before sundown

Dear Diary,

Our group is slowly gathering again... We are so stunned and confused! I'm thankful for these friends who are guiding us back to their home where we can feel safe; they are bringing us news from the city. Yesterday we barely knew them... and today they are precious friends and protectors. They tell us not to go out, since anyone with a Galilean accent who might have been seen with Jesus is brought to the authorities for questioning.

Evidently, late last night, there was a hastily-called council of the Sanhedrin.[1] Jesus was actually put on trial for being... for being... for being HIMSELF. From what we've heard, those testifying against Jesus couldn't even keep their stories straight.[2] Although much of the testimony contradicted itself and there was no corroborating evidence, the high priests found Jesus guilty of blasphemy. Jesus spent the rest of the night in the dreaded pit,[3] alone and in the dark, waiting to see what would happen. We heard tell that Peter was there, but we haven't heard any reports from him...

I really want to see the face of my master and friend again... to make sure he is all right and to beg for his forgiveness for falling asleep.

News on the street was that the religious authorities were planning to haul Jesus to stand before Pilate, so several of us crept over to Pontius Pilate's palace early this morning. I don't understand the policies, but it seems that no one can officially be put to death here in Jerusalem without the approval of the Romans. It was obvious that Pilate was irritated by his early wake-up call. He tried to release Jesus... he even tried to get the people to choose between Jesus and a notorious murderer, Barabbas, as the Passover "customary release".[4] It was really unbelievable when the crowd chose wicked Barabbas!! Then they started yelling that Pilate should have Jesus crucified. It was horrible!! I am sure that some of those people were the same ones who greeted Jesus so joyfully just last Sunday when he decided to come into the city on that donkey!

It seems that it was the SECOND time that Jesus faced Pilate. Somebody said that Pilate had earlier sent Jesus over to Herod's house. Herod is in Jerusalem for the Passover and since he is supposed to be the highest-ranking official of the Jewish government, evidently Pilate wanted Herod to take charge of this whole "Jesus matter". We're not sure exactly what happened, but we hear that Herod made fun of Jesus... and then sent him back to Pilate for a final decision.[5] So when Jesus failed to be the obvious "releasee" (as Pilate tried so hard), incredibly Pilate brought out a basin and right in front of everyone standing there, he washed his hands. How different from the basin that Jesus used at the Passover meal just last evening. Pilate shouted his claim that he thought Jesus was an innocent man and that he (Pilate) wasn't responsible for his death. I wish I had found my voice to shout out: "Of course, JESUS IS INNOCENT!!" but the words stuck in my heart. Oh, dear Jesus, please know that I love you and believe in you... but I confess that right now, I am a coward.

Everything started happening all too quickly![6] The soldiers whipped Jesus. Then they put a slinky purple robe on him and twisted thorns into a crown on his head and... they pretended to treat him like a king in sing-song mockery. They continued to make fun of Jesus as they made him carry a huge wooden cross all through the city streets out to Golgotha. The way was crowded with people... some were jeering at Jesus and others were crying. Jesus fell a couple of times... and for a while, a stranger picked out of the crowd carried the heavy cross.[7,8] I just wanted to run up to my Jesus, but strong arms held me back.

The place at Golgotha is called "Skull Hill". It really LOOKS like a human skull from a distance! There... they... they... they nai... they actually nailed His beautiful hands and feet to the cross. And they hung him there... right between two common criminals. Ohhhh, nooooo! I can't bear to describe it... but I can't get that awful picture out of my mind. They were killing my Lord! Ohhhhh.

John was there close by, alongside Jesus' mother, Mary. We couldn't hear a lot of what Jesus was saying; I hope John will remember it all to tell us later.[9]

It was over so fast[10]... Jesus died far more quickly than the two thieves hanging alongside him. The only time I heard Jesus' words was when he cried out to our G*d that "it is finished". It seemed that he was almost praying as he raised his head into the heavens and let out his last breath. I wanted it to stop!! I didn't want it to be "finished"! I wanted to wake up and see that it was all a horrible, horrible nightmare!

I'm not sure if the darkness around me was just in my head and heart... or if the sky really turned dark in the middle of day. My whole world seemed to rock and cave in... other people felt the earth shaking too.[11]

Again, strong arms pulled me away... I don't remember getting back to this house... the door is locked tight behind us.

Evidently, one of the religious leaders, Joseph of Arimathea,[12] has somehow taken charge of Jesus' body and made hasty preparations before sundown to put Jesus' remains into his own tomb in a garden just outside the city. Ohhh... our dear Jesus didn't even get a proper burial.

It's almost the beginning of the Sabbath and I must soon finish this entry. I am absolutely numb... it takes so much effort to write each letter. But maybe it doesn't matter if I cannot finish before sundown. I'm not sure I want to "keep the Sabbath"; nothing seems worth keeping anymore.[13]

11. Late after sundown on the Sabbath evening

Dear Diary,

The gloomy weather today reflects the gloom in my heart. Yes... we did observe the Sabbath with its sacred restrictions, more out of weariness than obedience. We are all so restless on this required "day of rest". We are waiting... in shock and silence. We are waiting... wishing to wake up from this horrific nightmare. We are waiting... wondering what we should do now that Jesus isn't here to guide us. I hate this empty waiting... for there seems to be no hope in any of it! I don't know who I am any more... I am no longer a "tag-along", since there is no one to follow after.

I feel so sorry for our dear companion, Simon Peter. Not that any of our actions were laudable last Thursday and yesterday, (oh my, was it only yesterday?) but Peter was one of the two disciples who was the brunt of a negative prediction at the Passover meal. Jesus declared that Peter would deny even knowing him and not only once, but multiple times. Maybe Jesus didn't point at me when he made that accusation, but I feel like I too denied knowing my dear Jesus when I abandoned him in the garden and failed to speak up from the crowd at Pilate's palace.

We now know that Peter followed Jesus to Caiaphas' house where the religious Sanhedrin meets[1]... he was there out in the courtyard during the mock trial that took place late that night. He's calling himself "Simon" again, because he doesn't think he deserves the name Peter (the rock) as Jesus named him.[2] He did, indeed, deny knowing Jesus... people outside saw him warming himself around the fires, and pointed fingers at him, recognizing his Galilean accent and thinking that they had seen him with the Lord on previous occasions. Peter (I mean Simon) was courageous enough to follow Jesus to Caiaphas' house, but there his bravado failed him, leading him to fail Jesus. Simon was so ashamed that he tried to hide, even from himself, during most of today's Sabbath day; friends found him huddled in a dark alley and helped him crawl back to where we ourselves have been hiding. We could hardly understand his confession amidst his tortured sobs. "Broken" doesn't begin to describe his appearance; he can barely stand, curled up in a ball, as he is. At least he came back to us. He fears that he will forever be known for his biggest hours of failure before Jesus. So he says he plans to head back to Capernaum to resume his fishing business... for him, it's the only thing that makes any sense now.

Those of us staying here together started talking about plans for some sort of burial and proper observance of our master's passing... but our sobs are too profound for any sort of plans.

We are still unsure as to whether Jesus' body will remain in the tomb of Joseph's family. By order of Pilate himself, there are soldiers guarding the tomb.[3] Do they honestly think that any of us would steal his body and pretend that he had come back from the dead, as Jesus said that he could?? Jesus' mother had hoped that the body could be transported to a more appropriate burial spot, but we doubt that we will be given permission to move it at this point. We hope that the soldiers will at least help roll the stone away from the front of the tomb so his body can be properly anointed. Jesus, of all people, deserves the smell of death to be covered, even just a little, by the anointing of spices. I wonder if ANY of the residue of Mary's recent pouring of nard over Jesus' head is still evident. We are nowhere near that garden tombsite; I cannot bear the thought that Jesus is buried alone without knowing how much we love him. I wonder what Lazarus would tell us about being buried alone in the darkness of death...

John has found his way back to us, too. He is in such shock... he just stares out from his sunken eyes. He keeps shaking his head, asking only for Mary, Jesus' mother. Of all the things that Jesus spoke while hanging on the cross,[4] John haltingly told us that Jesus told John to care for Mary, as if she were now his own mother. He cannot tell us of anything else; his grief is too deep for words or tears. I guess the rest of us are crying enough...

All Simon talks about is returning to Galilee to walk on the beach and to remember better times when Jesus was with the group. I don't know whether it's better to try to recall those good times and to share some of the events and stories that have been meaningful... or to try to put everything behind us as we imagine a new future... a new normal. Thoughts of Jesus make me smile a little... and then I remember the cruel reality that he has been taken from us. I hate this cruel and empty waiting!!

Our sister Mary Magdalene is organizing several of the faithful women in our group to bring spices to the tombsite as soon as the sun begins the day tomorrow morning. They will try to make sure his body is properly prepared. I hope they will be able to see a little more clearly through their tears and their weariness. This has been an exceedingly difficult day as we make plans.

Oh, how I wish it were different and we weren't talking about a funeral marking Jesus' death. I guess reality still hasn't quite fully hit me, because sometimes I imagine I can still hear his voice and his laugh and feel his gentle touch on my shoulder.

I feel so hopeless without Jesus! We have no plans... no ability... not even desire... to continue any of the work that Jesus talked about. What's the sense? Ohhh... Almighty... Are you there? If Jesus was truly your son, as he said he was... are YOU crying too? Surely, this can't be part of "the grand plan" for your great kingdom on earth, as Jesus often told us! Ohhh!

12. Early on the first day of the week

Dear Diary,

We are all in hiding, mourning each in our own way. We are mostly all here in this place, but we aren't really TOGETHER. We are all hurting so much that we can't comfort each other. It is quiet... too quiet.

Last evening, his mother Mary softly related the story of Jesus' birth when rich men traveled from the far east and brought precious gifts to Mary and Joseph and their little baby boy.[1] She recounted how she and Joseph had to trade the gold and frankincense to support themselves along the way, but that she, remarkably, had kept the large vial of myrrh all these years. Honestly, what kind of person brings myrrh as a gift for a baby?? Mary confessed she feared all through Jesus' life that the end would somehow come to this... it seems that when Jesus was just a baby, a wise man told her that her precious son would one day pierce her heart with great agony.[2] Although Mary is not prepared to face this reality, she isn't surprised... and she still has that large amount of myrrh to anoint her son.

After hearing that story, this morning was like a cruel twist of this nightmare! I don't suppose that Mary Magdalene, Jesus' mother, and Mary Salome[3] could sleep either, for it was still dark when I heard them leave. They were intent on going to the garden where Joseph of Arimathea's family tomb is situated. They carried the myrrh and other spices with them to anoint Jesus' body... even though he has been dead for two days, they still wanted to touch him once again and to wrap his burial clothes with oils and spices. They expressed their great concern of how to convince the Roman guards to open the tomb for them.[4]

Through our tears, we continue to try to plan some way to mark Jesus' funeral. It doesn't seem safe to do anything outside of our gathered group... but we just can't leave this death without proper public service of mourning. The disciples have tried so hard to lead the Kaddish prayers... those traditional words of our faith offered after the death of a loved one. They are meant to comfort, but when we get to the part praising G*d's greatness and G*d's plan for peace... our voices falter. What can we believe? HOW will we find any comfort in this horror??

STOP AND REFLECT

We know that Jesus agonized and died in a cruel way. Because we know the rest of the story, it is so easy to slip through the horrible, gory events of God's Friday without fully internalizing the impact of what Jesus endured. In these dark hours of early Sunday morning, take some time to reflect on what Jesus suffered.

---

13. Later on that first day of the week

Dear Diary,

To say that things have changed in the matters of hours is such an understatement!!

When the Marys returned from their planned task at the tomb... they were all three speaking at once... and their voices were so excited that their report was pretty jumbled as they practically fell over each other trying to relate what had happened. It was really hard to understand them.

It seems that the light of dawn was just creeping into view as they got closer to that garden tombsite.[1] They thought the trembling of the ground was simply a perception of the trembling of their hearts. Evidently by the time they reached the garden, there were no guards to be seen. The stone was rolled away from the door of the tomb, and as they looked in, they were devastated to see that the tomb was empty.

As they stood there at the open tomb, they saw angels... that's what they said... angels in dazzling white clothes who were sitting on the big stone that had sealed the entrance. The angels were singing that Jesus was not there... and they evidently thought it foolish of the women to be looking for a live person in the graveyard. The women ran back to us with that incredible report.

Leave it to the men to doubt that story. They thought the women must have been so hysterical in their grief and had wanted so much for Jesus not to be dead that they imagined such beings as angels. The women insisted that it wasn't simply their hearts' deepest desire, but that angels were REALLY there to tell them... (are you ready for this??) ... that Jesus had been raised from death and was ALIVE and WHOLE... just as he had said he would be!!

Of course, Simon had to see for himself. He went running and found that, indeed, the tomb was empty, except for the burial linens. Seeing those folded clothes still in the tomb indicated that the body had not simply been picked up and brought somewhere else... there was no dead body to be wrapped up.[2]

Simon then met Mary Magdalene[3] out there; she was beside herself with joy, for she HAD SEEN Jesus in person and actually TALKED WITH HIM! She was so excited that Simon could hardly understand what she was saying. She was shaking with emotion, but her eyes were clear and she said that Jesus stood right in front of her and spoke to her. By the time Simon talked with Mary, she was laughing at herself for mistaking Jesus for the gardener!!!

The news traveled fast; there are echoes all over the city. It started in low whispers behind closed doors... and then burst out into the streets. We hear that even the numerous Roman soldiers guarding the tomb can't seem to tell the same story, so we can't figure out what is true. How can we be sure?!? Is this really possible?? How can this news be verified?[4]

The early-morning whispers got louder and louder... and the whole city is alive with the news... I'll bet the whole world has heard it by now!

It IS true! We have seen the empty tomb for ourselves and we have heard the angels whisper and sing and shout!! We have laughed in the face of death and sin and pain and failure and sorrow and evil!!

The religious leaders and government officials had thought themselves so clever in that they had gotten rid of that nuisance from Galilee; that threat to their sacred boredom; that interruption in their holy routine... now even they are finding out that G*d's love is stronger than their holy alliances... that G*d's grace is greater than their little laws... that G*d's hope is bigger than their politically correct promises!! Ha ha hallelujah!!

I want to sing and shout "Hallelujah" and dance!! I am so excited, and I want to tell the whole world that Jesus is really alive... risen from the dead!!

I can't keep my quill point away from the exclamation points!!!!!! Ha ha ha hallelujah!!

Early this morning, we were huddling and hiding... all of us dead tired. Hmmmm. Interesting words: DEAD TIRED. We were tired from the horror of these last days and tired from the lack of sleep trying to make sense of it all. Then... then... then... we realized that Jesus is not dead, and we are not tired!!!! The brightness of G*d's glory has filled the sky and sparkled on our faces. The sweetness of G*d's love has filled our hearts. The majesty of G*d's miracles has colored our vision with truth.

Earlier we were trying to figure out how to properly honor and celebrate the past life of our teacher and leader... and now... we are awe-struck with the possibilities of truly CELEBRATING the NEW LIFE of our RISEN LORD! How do we spread this news? Can it be that there are those who haven't yet heard it!?!? Let the people who had walked through the dark sorrow of Saturday rejoice in the brightness of this Sunday!! Ha ha hallelujah!!!

STOP AND REFLECT

How do you celebrate the news that Jesus is alive? What difference does it make?

---

14. Monday... the day after Jesus' rising from the grave

Dear Diary,

It has all happened so fast that my head and my heart are still reeling! I keep pinching myself to make sure that it isn't a dream... and my pinches HURT every time! Just a few days ago, I was cursing G*d for raw feelings and now I am praising the Almighty for emotions and touch and the ability to feel.

We are putting pieces of the puzzle together as we talk to others and get more news.

The other day we feared that Judas had something to do with our master's arrest. Indeed, he did! We have no idea what motivated him or led him to that action... It seems inconceivable that Judas was against Jesus for any reason. When we remember Jesus' predictions as we gathered for the Passover meal just last Thursday, we know that Jesus knew somehow.

It seems that Judas received money for betraying our Lord.[1] There's talk that he tried to return it to the chief priests, but they would have nothing to do with so-called "blood money". Judas must have been desperate, for he killed himself sometime early Friday morning. How I wish he had left a note or something, so that we might know what he was thinking; all we can do is speculate.

He chose the most cursed way to kill himself.[2,3] Most desperate people fling themselves off the high pinnacle of the Temple into the deep ravine below, but Judas chose to hang himself, even knowing the ancient scriptural curse on anyone who hung from a tree. Perhaps he felt himself so unworthy that he figured he deserved yet another curse. I hope that I can someday pray for Judas' soul, but right now I am so angry at his actions, that I find it hard to feel sorry for him. He had been such a good friend and companion... what possibly could have led him??!??!

John is able to tell us little by little of the things that Jesus said to the crowd who watched him dying on the cross. One thing that Jesus uttered was: "Father, forgive them... for they don't know what they are doing".[4] I wonder if it would have made any difference to Judas to hear Jesus speak a word of forgiveness even as he was dying. I can only assume that Jesus' forgiveness was extended to even the one who betrayed him.

Ohhh... then my heart pounds and gets me to thinking that... hmmm... maybe I don't know exactly what I'm doing either, and that Jesus' words refer to me, too. It's so easy to point a finger of blame at someone else... oh... could it be that I should be able to forgive Judas? Oh, my dear Lord... forgive ME for my hesitancy and my unwillingness to extend forgiveness to the likes of Judas right now.

The message that Jesus left with Mary Magdalene was for her to tell us that he is heading to the Galilee and wants to meet us all there on the beach. HOW is that even possible?? Simon has said a couple of times that he planned to return to his fishing job there in Capernaum, but it seems that he has changed those plans; I think he is afraid and ashamed that he might have to face Jesus...

This time of celebration is still filled with so many conflicting feelings and thoughts. It's so hard to know what to do with this unbounded joy and the unresolved challenges, the love and the anger, the delight of our memories of Jesus and the fear for the future without him... I wish we could talk with Jesus again to ask some of these questions that are tearing at our hearts.

STOP AND REFLECT

Reflect on the different reactions of Judas and Peter to their failures.

15. Tuesday Evening... after the resurrection

Dear Diary,

The glorious news is still sinking in us and through us! It seems that even the birds are singing a different tune in these last few days! Jesus is alive and well! Jesus is alive and well! Jesus is alive and well! I can't help myself; I so love hearing that news that I keep repeating over and over again.

And the wonderful news continues to echo in grand ways. We were surprised that Cleopas came back to Jerusalem quite late Sunday evening.[1] He and his brother, Felix, had left us very early that morning to return home to Emmaus. In fact, they left so early that they had heard only a little bit of the reports of what the women thought they had seen at the tombsite. Cleopas and Felix both dismissed the women's words as foolish hysteria. (Ah, just like men!) They said they couldn't believe in those expressions of vain hope. We had tried to convince them to stay with us, but they were so upset (as were we all!) and simply wanted to leave the horror of that Friday on Golgotha behind them and return to their families. We were so worried that they might run into trouble on their day-long journey.

When Cleopas burst in, he was breathless, for he had run all the way back from his home. It was obvious from the gleam in his eyes that he has already heard the real news about Jesus. It was really funny, because we were all speaking at once! He said right off the bat that he didn't expect us to believe his story. I have never heard Cleopas speak so fast and so excitedly. I always thought him to be a somewhat boring speaker... usually so slow and deliberate!

He told us that as the two of them were walking back to Emmaus, they had their faces in the dust, their hearts deep in the shadow of despair... their hope in Jesus had come to a dead end. It seems that a stranger came up alongside them, and they were so broken-hearted that they didn't stop to think about WHERE the stranger might have come from.

The stranger broke into their quiet conversation to ask what they were talking about. Cleopas said that they both stopped short and asked if the stranger was the only person who didn't know of the terrible things that had happened in Jerusalem over the past few days. When the stranger pressed them for more information, the two couldn't believe that the stranger had heard nothing at all about Jesus the Nazarene. They proceeded to relate all that had happened in Jerusalem... as well as speaking of their hope that Jesus would be the one who would redeem all Israel. After they told the stranger the whole story, they were amazed to hear the stranger tell them things about the ancient scriptures that they never understood before.

As they approached their home in Emmaus, it seemed as if the man was going to continue his journey, but it was getting late and it would be thoughtless not to offer hospitality in their home. The stranger seemed to hesitate, but indeed consented to stay with them.

When they all sat down to eat supper, Cleopas invited the stranger to bless the bread (as was the custom). When the stranger broke the loaf and gave a piece to each person at the table, their eyes were opened to recognize that it was Jesus himself.... whole and alive... who had been walking with them... and who was RIGHT THERE in their home! As soon as they cried out in their excitement, Jesus disappeared from their sight.

Cleopas said that he and Felix just looked at each other... incredulous that they hadn't recognized Jesus earlier in the visit. Then Cleopas fell over himself trying to assure us that it wasn't simply a vision, for Jesus had really eaten some of the meal that they had offered to him. They couldn't imagine how they had missed his presence all the while they were walking along... after all, Jesus had opened the scriptures for them, and they had felt a strange burning in their hearts as he spoke.

Cleopas suddenly stopped recounting the story. He apologized for leaving Jerusalem... he apologized and asked our forgiveness! He felt terrible that he had turned his back on the truth by trying to run away. He now knew that Golgotha was not a place of failure, but of triumph! He had come back to Jerusalem as fast as he could to tell us the news... and found us celebrating.

It was late by the time Cleopas arrived... and by the time he finished his story and we got to tell him what had happened to us during the day, it was far late into the night. We realized that we were all famished, for in our excitement we hadn't eaten all day. When we all sat together at the table, sharing a meager meal, Cleopas cried out; "The bread. The broken loaf of bread! THAT's where we saw our Lord!! Don't you remember what he said the night of the Passover meal?? 'This is MY BODY, broken for you.'"

We ate together and our stomachs were satisfied... but much more, our very beings were filled with wonder and awe. I don't think I will ever look at a loaf of bread in the same way again. Some of the pieces are beginning to make sense. I hope we will get the chance to eat together often, remembering Jesus and this miracle of life and love...

As we reclined after eating, it was obvious that we wouldn't get much sleep. To be sure, we haven't had much sleep in the last week... for so many different reasons. But now, even as our eyes are begging for sleep, we were all too excited with the events of this day to settle down to rest. I keep looking at Cleopas and also at Mary Magdalene... how fortunate they have been to have seen our Lord on the very day that he was brought back to life. I do hope the rest of us will be so blessed as to meet Jesus in person.[2]

STOP AND REFLECT

Have you ever had the feeling that Jesus was somehow disguised in your presence and you didn't recognize Him?

---

16. Wednesday after the resurrection... Mary Magdalene

Dear Diary,

We can't believe the transformation in our sister, Mary Magdalene![1] She is absolutely glowing and is even more beautiful than I ever remembered her looking! Her eyes are clear and sparkling, having lost the haze of shame and grief. She doesn't walk around now; she dances as she moves, with a new grace and poise. It's amazing! None of us ever doubted her devotion to our Lord... but her love for him has manifested itself in her appearance. She is breathless with the realization that she was the first to SEE Jesus after his resurrection and actually SPEAK with him.

These days have been pure joy! What a difference in our whole outlook on LIFE this realization has made! Watching our dear friend Mary Magdalene dancing around has simply added to the awe of the news just a few days ago. Each time she retells her experience at the tomb makes our hearts thrill again.

Cleopas is still basking in the new-found understanding that his incredible encounter with Jesus has made. He has shared some of the insights that Jesus shared with him and Felix as they walked together. We too have felt our hearts burning as he has continued his story.

I confess that even as I rejoice with my friends here... I am a bit (dare I say it) jealous that they have had these incredible experiences with our living Jesus. I try to read the faces of the "chosen" disciples... it seems unfair that they (of all people) haven't seen and felt Jesus in the flesh. Hmmm... as I write those words "in the flesh", I am awed by the meaning of that phrase.

17. Thursday.. Jesus appears to the disciples

Dear Diary,

    The most marvelous news is that Jesus was really right here among us! It has only been a couple of days since that wonderful report of Jesus being ALIVE... my whole being absolutely tingles every time I think about it.

    It has been a wonderful, confusing, unbelievable, exciting, draining, and breath-taking time as we have tried to make sense of the fact that the tomb was empty and there were messages from angels telling us not to look for Jesus in a graveyard, but among the living. We are awe-struck by the accounts of Mary Magdalene and Cleopas. I thank G*d that so many of us are still together as we sing and praise this good news. We still laugh when we look back at what started out as a FUNERAL on that first day of the week ended being such a glorious CELEBRATION OF LIFE!!! We were still putting together bits and pieces of news from all parts of the city.

    THEN... After we had all somewhat settled down last evening and we had closed the doors and windows against the night and against all the deadly forces that couldn't and wouldn't celebrate our Lord's restored life... all of a sudden... Jesus was there![1] He didn't exactly COME IN; he didn't mysteriously APPEAR through a wall... I can't quite explain it... but there he stood with us... healthy and whole and ALIVE!

    We were excited and dazed at the same time; none of us was quite sure exactly what to do or how to react. He looked at us and pronounced his blessing. "Peace be with you!"

    Peace! I remember him saying (oh, that seems so long ago!) that the peace he could give us was nothing like any peace that we had ever known on this earth. When he told us not to let our hearts be troubled or afraid, I never imagined that there would be a time that I would feel as scared as I do now. To be sure, none of us is really sure WHAT we fear, but all this is all pretty frightening! That is, until Jesus stood there and blessed us with his peace. It was so wonderful! It was like a giant cloud filled the room with comfort and grace and assurance. My heart was still trembling and tingling, but it was a different sort of trembling. Is there such a thing as "sacred trembling"???

There was mighty shaking and rejoicing as we gathered there... Jesus right there with us! I have never been so happy... no... it surpasses happiness... I have never been so joyous... no!... it surpasses that, too, but I don't know another word for it. Perhaps we will have to learn a whole new set of words and feelings... and I wonder if that time will be on THIS side of our promised eternal heaven. We are all beginning to more fully understand many of the things that Jesus tried to teach us for all these past months and years.

Jesus repeated his blessing of true peace and then he said that WE would be sent just as he was sent to us. I have to tell you, the "buzz" in that room stopped short! Sent, Lord?? Excuse me! SENT?? Sent WHERE? ALL OF US?? WHEN? ME?? HOW??? To do WHAT???

I don't know what to do with this new feeling in me... I can't even identify it... hmmm... it's not DREAD... but it seems to have an edge of FEAR... Does Jesus' admonition of not being afraid also reach out to calm this "HOLY TREPIDATION"? Are we really feeling the awesome "fear of the Lord" that the ancient Psalmists sang about?

Jesus calmed our unvoiced questions with a sweep of his gaze and then... then... gosh, I am not sure how to describe what happened. He breathed on us... INTO us, really... and told us to receive the "Holy Spirit". I couldn't catch my breath... it was like a strong wind in my face that made me inhale, inhale, inhale, inhale, inhale... until I thought my lungs would burst! But there was no WIND and it wasn't my LUNGS that couldn't catch more breath...

As quickly and quietly as Jesus came into our midst... he wasn't there anymore.

Oh dear, I can't find the words to explain this very well; I have never experienced anything like this in my life. The wide eyes of everyone else in the room told me that we all had experienced the same thing! I only wish that more people could have been there to be part of it. I can't believe that we are the only ones that Jesus will touch like this. I only hope that Jesus will manifest himself to many others too. Even as I write these words, I'm not sure how I can share this experience with other people... surely, we are not supposed to keep this knowledge to ourselves...

HOW are we to share the ways that Jesus has touched our hearts in such profound ways? HOW are we to continue Jesus' legacy of touching and healing? HOW might we bear witness to the difference that Jesus has made in the lives of so many people he has touched? We looked around this place for objects that Jesus might have held... thinking that we could use those things to open conversations with others. Do we keep those objects and give them a special place here and use them ONLY as foci of our worship? WHAT did he actually touch? What about the cup that he held during that last Passover feast? Are those burial linens so carefully laid aside still available? As soon as this idea was discussed, it was dismissed... Jesus cannot be defined by such relics. Surely, we will need new conversation-openers for this fantastic message of LIFE!

The reality of what I am trying to record seems so SURREAL! How could all of this have happened exactly as Jesus said it would? He spoke often of his Father's plan... I'm beginning to think that all the pain and death and grief and darkness and fear and dread were somehow necessary to get to this present point of unsurpassed joy.

I think I know now why he seemed so frustrated with us just a week ago... he sensed that we had no idea... not even a CLUE about facing the events that would happen. We all wish we had paid more attention... or had had more time to ask questions. Yet, I'm not even sure we could have imagined what questions to formulate.

As wonderful as all this has been, there is daily work to do. We still must eat and sleep and do the chores necessary to live. The "chosen" men aren't highly educated, but they seem to be... "trainable". They are strong and capable in many ways, but they are fairly helpless to make their own meals and care for their own clothes. It's a good thing that Jesus has allowed us women to tag along with this special group. It's easier and less conspicuous for us women to go outside for necessary supplies... and NO, the men don't want to stand out by fetching water for our large group. So, our women's work is important, albeit pretty mundane.

I wonder if we are somehow missing something right in front of us as we try to decipher the unfolding of our future.

18. Early Friday evening... before the Sabbath begins

Dear Diary,

What a difference in our current Sabbath from last week![1]

It has been only one week... seven days... each filled to overflowing with such different events and emotions. This one single week has seemed almost like a LIFETIME. I can't fathom what ETERNITY promises for us.

It seems more difficult to write sometimes; there were times when words failed. When we were confused and hurting so, the depths of our grief were so profound that we were each in little personal bubbles... it was so SOLITARY... which made the hurt even more profound. Now... we are constantly singing and dancing in our jubilation... and it's so much more COMMUNAL! We are always touching and hugging... even as we are still trying to make sense of it all.

Last week, we couldn't sleep what with the sounds of nails pounding and of wailing haunting our thoughts... what with even more profound shadows of uncertainty and danger piercing the darkness... what with the smell of death surrounding us even though we were distant from the graveyard... what with the taste of bile in our throats even when we tried to eat something that we women prepared to nourish us all... what with the turmoil of hopelessness and emptiness tearing into our hearts. Now... we don't sleep for the sound of laughter and all the times we pop up to remember something that Jesus said that didn't make sense at the time, but now we understand better what he was trying to tell us.

As I write Jesus' name, I have a new sense of who He was... and still IS. I don't know how to express that in my words... and I have decided to use a capital letter when referring to Him. I'm ashamed that it has taken me so long to realize His true identity... yet I'm grateful that I have lived long enough to proclaim that I have personally known the promised Messiah. I have seen Him with my own eyes... and I've had the grand privilege to be a "tag-along"!

Dear Hannah is setting out the Sabbath candles and calling us to observance. Last week, I didn't see the point of keeping our G*d's Sabbath... on this day, there is so much to keep precious and holy that I don't know how we will fit it all in.

STOP AND REFLECT

"Keeping the Sabbath" takes on a different meaning for the followers; how do YOU keep Sabbath holy?

The diarist decides to use a capital H when referring to Jesus. How would YOU indicate your understanding of Jesus? Would you use a different name or designation?

19. Sunday... a week after the resurrection

Dear Diary,

Yesterday was another day of Sabbath rest. Some of our group felt safe enough to go up to the Temple to pray. They reported such confusion in that area... it would have been laughable if it weren't so sad. The Temple leaders were trying hard to quell the "rumors" of the appearance of the promised Messiah.

Evidently, there are conflicting reports given by the Roman soldiers who were ordered to guard the tomb.[1] Some admitted that they had all fallen asleep and didn't see anything unusual until the women woke them asking to roll the stone away... and by then, the body was missing. Others claimed they were attacked by a large group of disciples who had stolen the body. No matter what story those soldiers come up with, they aren't believable... and they are in big trouble. I hardly feel sorry for them!

At the same time, the religious authorities are telling the people that the reports of "appearances" of the "living" Jesus are pure fabrications. They still seem pretty smug that they have managed to kill Jesus and that the problem He presented has been "solved".

I wonder how long it will be before even those religious men will begin to see the truth in what the Almighty has done for everyone. Now, I'm not sure we can trust ANYTHING that those leaders have to tell us...[2,3]

We observed the Sabbath as we have been accustomed to doing all our lives. At the same time, we are struggling with the notion of things Jesus said about a "new day" and a "new hope" and what all that might mean about our worship. So, we decided together that we will also gather specifically for worship on this first day of the week, because it was on this day that our lives were transformed as Jesus was resurrected from the dead. We sing praises to the Almighty and we reaffirm our belief that Jesus is our Messiah and Savior. One of the most moving parts of our first-day gathering has been the sharing of bread, remembering what Jesus told us that night of the Passover meal... and about the witness of Cleopas recognizing Jesus in that breaking of bread.

It is new and exciting... yet we want to be assured that we are walking in the path of light and life, as would please Jesus. We yearn to see Him again... and perhaps ask Him to show us more clearly the way we should walk and live.

STOP AND REFLECT

The followers feel something special in the breaking of bread together. Can you remember significant celebration of Communion?

20. Monday... retelling the stories

Dear Diary,

     I have to say that it has been a strange week as we all struggle to find our place in this topsy-turvy world.[1]

     While we are together, we retell all the stories and incidents that we experienced with Jesus during the time we were with Him. We are trying so hard to remember exactly what He said at certain times. It's interesting to hear the different viewpoints... there are times that we were at the very same event, yet we have such varying recollections! It's amazing that we remember such different things!

     Mark is expressing his desire to write all these stories down, so there will be an accurate record of the events and sayings of Jesus during His ministry.[2] I know how hard it has been for me to write in this diary shortly after the events have unfolded... we are already recalling different words and different highlights. I can't imagine how Mark can think of depending on our memories over the period of months and even years. And HOW could that magnitude of material be maintained if Mark could ever manage to write all that down!?!

     I don't mind repeating that although there is an incredible joy to know that our Lord is alive, there is still an indescribable fear lurking in our lives. Especially the "chosen" who are more easily known for having travelled with Jesus, few of us dare to leave this safe place unless we really have to... and even then, we don't travel as a group larger than two, maybe three of us. The biggest difficulty is buying things we need, because we don't want to talk a lot, lest we be betrayed by our recognizable Galilean accents. Jesus has told us that we have nothing to fear, but it is difficult to live when there are still so many threats "out there". When we leave the house, we pull our hoods and scarves well over our heads, so to hide our faces. How long will we have to live like this?

21. Visit from Roman soldier

Dear Diary,

We had a great scare several evenings ago. There was a knock at the door, but we were all already inside. The knock came again... we hardly dared to breathe for fear of opening the door. Then a voice on the other side pleaded with us to open the door, adding that he had no intention of harming us. The voice said he really needed to speak with us... that he wanted to talk about our friend, Jesus.

Imagine our surprise... and fear... when we opened the door a crack and came face to face with a Roman soldier... in full uniform, but with no weapon. He sank to one knee and begged us to let him enter.

"How did you find us?" we asked, fearing that if HE could find us, surely other less well-meaning soldiers could also find us!! He said that he hoped we were still in the vicinity and that he had been watching closely in the last days to catch a glimpse of one of us that he might speak with us. He said he saw us in the street (remember, wearing a deep hood over our heads that we thought cleverly shadowed our faces) and he assumed by the shine in our faces that radiated out from deep within the cowl that we were followers of the King Jesus.

As he told us his story, we found out that he had been assigned to command the crucifixion detail on that Friday (it seems like ages ago). He told us it was the first time he had ever felt uneasy about carrying out orders. He thought there was SOMETHING about Jesus that set Him apart from ANYONE he had ever set eyes on. He said he knew Jesus was exactly who the religious leaders feared He was, especially when Jesus gave in to sweet death so quickly. As a soldier, he was trained never to give up the fight... but as he stood there looking at Jesus on the cross, he felt that Jesus wasn't giving UP but rather giving IN to something far greater than he ever knew existed.

Suddenly, John approached the soldier and asked him if he were the soldier who had stood right there at the foot of the cross and cried out that Jesus was truly the Son of G*d.[1] Again, the soldier sank to his knees and silently nodded. John turned around to us and, with wonder in his voice, declared that indeed, this soldier was the FIRST to recognize the true identity of our Lord Jesus... just minutes after His death.

As the Roman commander continued his story, we found out that he was also in the garden leading the detail guarding the tomb early that Sunday morning. He had felt the earthquake and then saw the light coming from INSIDE the tomb that was suddenly opened. He said he stood there while the other soldiers ran away, knowing that their jobs, and perhaps their lives, were in jeopardy. But he just stood there and remembered all the things that the mocking religious leaders had said about this Jesus... and he said the truth of all that had happened was reinforced in his heart.

The soldier knows now that he cannot stay in the Roman army... but he isn't sure what he will do. He asked if we had any ideas. He wanted to know more about Jesus and if it was true that we had really seen Him.

We spent the entire night talking with him, telling him as many stories and words as time would allow. Wow! What a joy it was to see the change in this man as he heard our stories! He asked thoughtful questions and listened carefully as the stories tripped out of our memories and through our lips!

After spending the whole night talking, you would have thought we'd be tired... but we were so energized!!! I wonder if we will ever get another chance like this to talk with others who have not met Jesus personally. THAT would be interesting "work" to do...

We are trying so hard to be at peace with one another... but frankly... being cooped up together is pretty exasperating. At times, we are getting on each other's nerves, as we try to process all these new and unbelievable experiences, while at the same time, our future is STILL such an unknown entity.

STOP AND REFLECT

Is there a person barely mentioned in scripture that you wish you could know more about? What story would YOU tell?

22. Centurion and companion return with Jesus' cloak

Dear Diary,

MY GOODNESS! There are so many surprises and unintended consequences happening around us.

We recognized the voice after the rap on the door... it was the Roman centurion who had come the other evening. "Please... allow us to enter." Us? US?? We held our collective breaths as we cracked open the door. There again... in full regalia was that soldier, together with another in full armor... and again, NO WEAPONS.

They came in. In reality, the unknown soldier fairly crawled in, with his head cast down, his body almost folded in half. "Thank you! This man... really BOTH of us... we need your help." It was then that we saw that the companion was carrying a robe that we all recognized as the robe that our Jesus had worn.

"Please take this back," sobbed the soldier. It took a while for us to understand his story. He too had been assigned to the crucifixion detail. As Jesus was dying, the soldiers there had continued to loudly mock him. They had stripped Jesus of all His clothes, dividing those items among the soldiers in the detail. When they came to His robe, they realized that it was a perfect garment, seamlessly woven in one piece from top to bottom. Rather than rip the robe apart, they decided to cast lots and award it to the winner.[1]

Initially, the centurion was delighted... what good luck to have won the toss of lots![2] He took the garment home... and almost immediately "things" started happening... his wife dropped and broke a large water jar spilling all the fetched water, their three chickens escaped their pen, and his son became deathly ill.

A little later, after admiring the new cloak won during the day's work, his wife felt an ominous cloud in their home. "Take that thing out of here!" she begged her husband, adding that she had a sense that it was cursed. Her husband tried to quell her foolish fears, but he was quickly haunted by the same feeling. He rolled up the garment in a back corner of the alley behind their quarters, intending to throw it out the next day.

It was then that the centurion met the Roman soldier, who cautiously told of his visit with us. Together, the two centurions decided to return to us, hoping that we would be willing to take the cloak and perhaps forgive them... for, as Jesus had said from the cross: "... they don't know what they are doing".

By the time the two soldiers got to this point in telling their story, they were both sobbing uncontrollably. They pleaded, "Can you forgive even us? Can you take this curse from us? Can you... will you bless us, after all that we have done?"

The intense silence filled the room. John was the first to find his voice. "We can forgive you... especially since you have been instruments to fulfill some of the ancient prophecies. But we cannot take away the curse and give you a blessing." The soldiers crumbled into balls on the floor as they heard those words.

But WAIT!! John kept speaking! "We do not have the authority to turn curses into blessings... but we do know that our great G*d has that ability. We believe that G*d can, and will, extend that grace to you in the name of our Risen Lord, Jesus Christ."

Slowly, first John and then the other disciples moved forward to help the soldiers stand up and to wipe the tears from their faces. Someone started singing very softly.

The soldiers looked at us and at each other. They began stripping until they were standing there in their undergarments. There were three piles on the floor in front of us: two heaps of Roman uniforms... and a blessed robe.

I have no more words.

23. Two weeks after resurrection... Jesus appears while Thomas is present

Dear Diary,

We continue to live out the glory and grace of our RISEN LORD. But I have to admit, the shine of glory sadly seems to be tarnishing a tad bit.

Although we are not sure WHAT the future holds for us all, we are holding tightly to the assurance of WHO holds our future! We are living in the hope that Jesus will continue to guide us and empower us for the work He began and wants us to continue.

During these last several weeks, we have endeavored to keep talking and marveling, singing and praising, wondering and... going through all sorts of possible plans, saying "what IF...?" We are in awe of the glory of G*d that our Master Jesus is alive and whole and can appear into our midst at will... well, at HIS will, not ours. As much as we pray together for His actual presence among us, He appears only infrequently when He wills. Are there lessons for us in this waiting? Is there something that we have missed that would make this waiting more tolerable... and perhaps even profitable?

Evidently, Jesus wanted to be with us again yesterday on the first day of the week. When He appeared last week and took our breath away with His presence and just as quickly filled us with a different breath... well, at that time, our friend and companion, Thomas, was not with us.

When we told Thomas what had happened, his face clouded and his whole body shook. It was almost a growl that emerged from his lips as he declared that he could not believe the "nonsense" that we talked about. Surely, he said, this whole episode was just "wishful thinking". No one wanted Jesus to be with us any more than Thomas, but being the practical man that he is, he countered that we had to face the facts, no matter how grim and ugly those facts were. Surely the women were overwrought and strained when they were at the tomb site in the gray darkness just before dawn. Surely, the disciples were hallucinating out of frayed nerves and longing for what never could be!

Thomas is sure that Mary Magdalene's report that Jesus warned her NOT to touch Him really PROVED that He was nothing more than a ghost... not to be held, lest it be less than a solid body. Thomas loudly declared that he could not believe in these stories of a vision who suddenly appeared out of nowhere. NO! He needed to feel solid flesh and bones. Thomas declared that until he himself could see the Lord with his own eyes and put his own hands into the wounds in Jesus' hands and feet and feel the wound in Jesus' side... THEN, and ONLY THEN could he believe for himself.[1]

I was surprised at Thomas' outburst. How could he NOT believe the truth when so many of us had seen Jesus and knew for sure that He was alive? But there were a few of the gathered who moved next to Thomas and haltingly admitted that they too, had wondered how (and even IF) this wonderfully absurd story was really true... but they were afraid to admit that, for fear that they would be condemned by the group and cast out as "unbelievers." I guess I hadn't really looked at Thomas' admission of doubt as an honest expression of his faith needing to be tested.

A time of quiet came over our group as we sat together wondering about this latest twist... does honest doubt have any part of our faith journey?

We had little time to think about all that when Jesus again appeared among us. He must have been listening to this whole conversation because He immediately went to Thomas and stretched out His hands for Thomas to touch Him.

I remember thinking that His hands had scars on them... SCARS, not wounds. Jesus' hands were completely healed of the wounds and only the scars remained! He was healed, but still bore the ugly marks of the weight that He carried. Ohhhh, as quickly as I pictured that in my mind, I tried to pull that thought back... I scared myself thinking that there was ANYTHING ugly about my Jesus. But there they were, right out there for everybody to see... UGLY SCARS.

Jesus stood there with His hands out and dared... no, not only dared, INVITED, well, no, not even invited... URGED, yes urged Thomas to touch Him. I don't know what Thomas was thinking or feeling... he was still so moved with emotion that he could barely squeak out a word. He quickly bent over as if ashamed and humbled by the living Jesus before him. He had barely traced those scars with his finger when, just as suddenly, his eyes bulged out and his chest swelled until it looked like Thomas would burst. The words shot out of his mouth: "MY LORD and MY G*D!!!"

There was a look of compassionate pride on Jesus' face as He put His hand on Thomas' shoulder and said, "Because you have seen Me, you have believed." Then His face changed, and it seemed that He was speaking ABOVE Thomas rather than AT him, as He continued: "Blessed are those who have not seen Me and yet still believe."

I don't think that Jesus was chastising Thomas... hmmm. Something tells me that in days to come, we will all look back at this event and it will be clear what Jesus meant. I think that Thomas' doubt will help us all to believe more completely. We are all realizing that there's no shame in questions, in doubts, or desiring some form of PROOF. As we continue this journey with our resurrected Lord... even as we yearn to become strong and courageous followers... I see that we still need to poke the wounds and see for ourselves. And I wonder... how much solid proof will we need to solidly believe? Is this what "faith" is all about?

Right now, I stand amazed that Jesus knows exactly what each of us needs in order to believe the truth... and He works diligently to fill that particular need. I wonder what He has in store for the rest of us. As for me, I cannot begin to identify exactly what I need... but I trust that my Jesus knows... and I pray that I will understand and have the courage to follow His direction when it comes.

There is still some discussion that the disciples should be returning to the Galilee...

STOP AND REFLECT

Have you had the experience of being touched (or prayer answered) in the unique way that YOU needed? Thomas is known as "the doubter". Would you give him a different nickname?

24. Thursday afternoon several weeks after the
    resurrection... Joseph of Arimathea

Dear Diary,

This has been such a strange time. We are all together, mostly staying inside where we feel safe. There isn't much private time to sit and think and write. My emotions are so jumbled that I'm not quite sure how to identify what I'm feeling and thinking to write all this out.

The other evening, we had a visit from Joseph of Arimathea. We had so wanted to talk with him about the events surrounding our Lord's burial, but we weren't sure if Joseph was in any danger or if he even wanted to talk with us. Well, come to find out... he hesitated to contact us for the very same fears!

We knew that Joseph is (or was) a member of the Sanhedrin, so his actions gave us much pause for wonder.[1] After we heard the whole story, we find out that his colleagues were aware of his sympathies and affinity for Jesus. Previously, Joseph had disagreed with his colleagues several times when they discussed the "threat" that Jesus posed for the religious authorities in Jerusalem. Knowing that, it was decided to conveniently not notify Joseph of the extraordinary meeting that was hastily called on that Thursday night after Jesus was arrested in the garden. Joseph knew that Nicodemus had tried to persuade the others that Jesus was innocent and holy, but the Sanhedrin had decided their verdict long before Jesus appeared before them. Joseph couldn't believe the shameful performance of the religious authorities.

Joseph's chest tightened and his words came out painfully slow as he told us that he was among those present at the crucifixion and just couldn't believe that the Messiah and the dreams of generations of Hebrew people were on the verge of dying.

He told us that he prayed hard before going to Pilate to ask for Jesus' broken body.[2] He had so wanted to believe that Jesus was the Messiah, and he didn't want any more damage done to that precious body that had already been beaten and pierced. He felt that the high holy days of Passover had already been sullied, so he didn't want an unburied body to further defile the holiday.

Joseph admitted that he was somewhat timid until the very moment that he stood before Pilate to request Jesus' body. It was quite obvious that Pilate also wanted to be finished with all that "Jesus stuff" and didn't ask many questions before he gave Joseph the permission he needed to take care of the body. Evidently the only thing that Pilate said was that he couldn't believe that one of the religious leaders would dare to come and ask for the body.

All the time Joseph was talking with us, he kept repeating "I just couldn't believe it was happening..."

Joseph said he never knew what had possessed him months earlier to prepare a grave in Jerusalem... after all, his entire family is from Arimathea, two days' journey away from Jerusalem. He said that he felt privileged that he had the place right near Golgotha Hill that could be used quickly as the minutes slipped away that Friday afternoon before sundown marking the beginning of the Sabbath.

As Joseph and Nicodemus hurriedly prepared the body, they knew they would incur the resentment of all the other Jewish leaders and perhaps of all the people they served. They didn't have the luxury to take the time to count the consequences at that moment. Joseph said they did what they had to do without saying too much to each other; perhaps neither could believe what the other one was doing. Nicodemus had spent some precious time buying some nard to wrap in the burial linens, which made their preparations even more hurried.[3] The two did what was possible as they hastily wrapped Jesus' body. In those moments as the sun was quickly slipping nearer to the horizon, each of them should have been making joyful last-minute preparations with his family... yet, there they were... in danger of defiling themselves for Jesus' sake.

Both Joseph and Nicodemus found some comfort in that kindly deed that they were hurriedly performing. Even as they were speaking, neither of them can believe that G*d had given them that small, yet important task... little could the two men have known that the act of burying Jesus' body would change history within a few days.

Joseph really needed to talk with us about his feelings and his future. He just kept repeating "I can't believe I actually did that." He hasn't been back to face his Jewish colleagues... he says he is not sure what he thinks or believes about their work and influence in the religious life of the people...

I don't know if there is such a thing as a "crisis of faith", but if there were, Joseph is having one right now. He doesn't know whether he has a future within the Jewish religious establishment. Will there be any change among the religious authorities if the likes of Joseph aren't allowed to speak freely from within their company? Will he be allowed... or accepted?? Can he work for change from the outside without facing the same threats and consequences as Jesus? We talked about his joining with us... and he isn't sure of that, either. He has family responsibilities to think about, after all.

He sat with us for hours, shaking his head and repeating that he couldn't believe the events as they unfolded. Mixed in with his story were so many accounts of "co-incidences" that G*d MUST have orchestrated for everything to ultimately unfold as it did. Joseph related many little bits of scripture that seemed to foretell the events that we have lived through. It still gives me shivers of hope to remember Joseph's story... especially now that we can see all those events and all the aspects of ancient prophecy through the lens of our Lord's resurrection...

As Joseph prepared to leave us, a warm silence fell over the whole group. We had told Joseph that we had actually seen the Lord... and his reaction was so memorable. "THAT I CAN believe," he said. "Yes, now I CAN BELIEVE. I can believe that G*d still keeps promises!"

I hope that, somehow, we can all grasp that fragile truth... and that we can truly BELIEVE that G*d has a mighty plan for each of us, even though we aren't sure of what it is!

With Joseph's visit, I think we all realize that there is something very precious in our small community of ... of... yes, I'll use the word... this community of BELIEVERS... believers in the glory of our risen Jesus and the wonderful plan of our G*d for us. We need to take care of each other! In spite of the uncertainty of our days, we need to call each other to the awareness of the ways G*d is working around us.

STOP AND REFLECT

When has God unexpectedly put an idea or action into your heart that completely turned your life around? How can you react without fully understanding?

25. Questions

Dear Diary,

All of us are trying so hard to stay together and to remain joyful despite the weariness of being cooped up in this place.[1] We are safe here... safe at least from the threats of the religious authorities and the control of the Romans on which they depend. Right now, the biggest danger seems simply being here together. We try to sing joyfully, remembering our incredible LIVING Lord Jesus. But the little complaints sometimes tend to overshadow our songs. One person just can't stand to sing "that song" even one more time, yet that same song is the one that speaks directly to another's heart. Some are tired of repeating over and over the same prayers that have been part of our tradition for generations. We need to better learn how fearful and weary hearts can rejoice!

It used to worry me that some strangers can identify us when we are hiding away from the authorities... but the soldiers and religious leaders who could do us harm never seem to come to our door or even confront us in the marketplace (although there are constant rumors that they are really angry at the ways they were humiliated by Jesus' return from the dead). I've come to realize that that's THEIR problem, not ours.

The eleven disciples of Jesus' choosing are the most vulnerable if they go outside, but they are caught in such an uncomfortable situation... they are so very restless in here, and yet they are hesitant to leave.

We women are somewhat freer to go about. And leave we must in order to get provisions and water for us all. It's getting more and more difficult to navigate without meeting people asking if we are among the believers of Jesus. We are never sure why they are asking. Are they seekers curious to hear more about Jesus? OR... are they seekers eager to earn a bounty that is surely offered for information about us? Are we being unnecessarily paranoid?

There have been several people who have stopped us in the marketplace, wanting to talk about Jesus and His "Father G*d". They say they know us by the shine in our faces. Hmmm... I guess it's a good thing that at least we are still shining the good news of our living Jesus.

Some of them report that, in some way, they had been personally touched by Jesus during His ministry... either by His words or by His healing. They are eager to know how they can join our group of believers. Oh, my Lord, are we supposed to crowd even more people into our hiding place? Do we invite others to worship with us? Could this be an indication that we should be moving somewhere else?

There are others who are seeking miracles from us, as Jesus was known to perform for others. Oh, Jesus, help us... we don't have your powerful ability!

One woman whose husband had died, had a specific question: "I want to know how to believe so he will live again." Well... YES!! But... hmmm... no, it's different. Hmmm... None of us knows how to explain.

Another stranger asked: "Are we to be baptized, like that man, John, proclaimed some time ago?"[2]

Each time we hear a question, many more questions well up within us. By what authority do we even try to answer the questions of those seekers?? WHO are WE to guide others who question... and HOW do we baptize other believers (and is that even something we are supposed to do)? Sometimes strangers articulate questions we didn't even know we had. As many other people seek us out, we realize that we are ALL seeking together... in different ways. Even though we like to think that we are further along in our journey, we too are still seeking. So many questions! I don't think any of us feels worthy or capable. Lord Jesus, show us your answers! Guide us!

I dared not articulate my questions and apprehensions. Then I remembered the several among us who dared reveal their doubts ONLY after Thomas had the courage to utter his own. Even as I hesitated to pose my own queries, I was amazed when someone ELSE shared MY same questions... and dared to voice them out loud. After a long silence, several others nodded.

In response, Luke and John usually close their eyes... breathe deeply... think carefully... before speaking. They have offered some examples of questions and conundrums from our ancient scriptures. They reminded us that, through the generations, when our G*d had called people to do specific tasks... the first response out of the mouths of those being tasked was an excuse.[3] Moses couldn't speak well. Isaiah thought himself too unclean. Jeremiah was sure he was too young. Jonah was so scared that he ran in the other direction. Even, as we remembered... our Lord, at the time He was facing imminent death on our behalf, asked the agonizing question: "ABBA, G*D, WHY HAVE YOU FORSAKEN ME?"

How will our G*d ever manage to touch us with the answers we so desperately need? Oh, dear Almighty, are we even asking the right questions?

STOP AND REFLECT

What questions and fears roll around in your heart and head? What keeps you from articulating all those important questions?

26. A voice in the marketplace

Dear Diary,

Even as we were beginning to feel a little more comfortable going outside with the "threat" of those unexpected encounters, today's experience really set several of the women on edge. They were SO upset that they returned from the marketplace without buying the needed things. They were breathless when they admitted that they had seen THAT MAN again. They didn't have to say much more, because this news is not new.

We have heard numerous reports about this rugged man who stands up near the entrance of the market, and we have heard him ourselves a couple of times. It seems that he is getting more and more vocal about his encounter with our Jesus... and how that has changed him so completely. By now, the women recognize his voice even before seeing him. But today, it was different... because the man had a young boy right next to him.

His story has become familiar. The man speaks loudly about being a prisoner of the Romans at the time of the Passover. He knew he was guilty of terrible crimes and was destined to die. From his cell, he heard the shouts "crucify him!" from the crowds outside and figured that his end was near. He thought the guards were mocking him when they opened his cell and told him that it must be his lucky day. He was jostled up onto the platform where Pontius Pilate was trying to speak with the crowds below them. He hadn't noticed the man standing on Pilate's other side. He DID hear when the crowd shouted his name: "BARABBAS" and he thought that was his death sentence.[1] But he was surprised when the guards untied the ropes binding his hands and neck and told him to "go home... if you have a home".

Day after day, the rough-looking man has been telling the gathered shoppers in the market that he wandered around Jerusalem for a while after being released before he noticed that the crowds were rushing along the narrow streets toward the city gates. When he asked what was going on; one in the crowd quickly answered: "It was supposed to be some criminal named Barabbas, but the governor let him go. So they're going to crucify that Jesus guy who pretended to be the Messiah. Hurry up, or we'll be late."

Barabbas recounts that he was swept up in the crowd until it came to the hill called Golgotha. There he remembers a frightening sight... three crosses were silhouetted against the sky. Barabbas dared to edge closer to get a better look at the man who was dying instead of him. Just as he got near to the front of the crowd, he saw the cracked lips begin to move, and he heard those incredible words, "Father, forgive them, for they don't know what they are doing."

Barabbas speaks of the feeling a punch in his gut, "That man was dying for me. I was supposed to be up there on that cross." Barabbas now freely tells the marketgoers that on that day, one man died, and another lived. And now that Barabbas has heard the news of Jesus coming back to life, he realizes that maybe, in the long term... it's the other way around.

What really alarmed the women today was that Barabbas' talk went further than it ever had in the past. He acknowledged that he had never been educated and didn't speak well. He said that he used to be proud of the foul way that he spoke to everyone. He confessed that he had never before given a thought about right or wrong when faced with someone who had the money or item that he wanted. He even cringed a little when he related that he wasn't proud that he had regularly surrounded himself with "friends" who found great pleasure at seeing which of them could be the grossest, the meanest, the most violent. Evidently his voice softened when he said that the idea of "family" was foreign, but he had come to recognize that the child standing there with him was his son. Barabbas told those in the marketplace that his near encounter with Jesus has made him realize that he must be responsible to himself, so he could be responsible to that young boy and for his mother. Barabbas loudly proclaimed that he needed people to see that he was a changed man because of Jesus.

What really upset the women wasn't so much the story that Barabbas told there, but that he seemed to think that he had some right to speak repeatedly about our Jesus, even though he wasn't among "the chosen"... or even a "tag-along" who had known Jesus much better.

"Shouldn't he be stopped??" the women asked.

In the silence that followed, Mark and John stared at each other, and John whispered: "Help me remember what Jesus said that day."

Mark started recounting a time quite a while ago when the disciples were coming together and complaining to Jesus that they had seen a man driving out demons, lifting up Jesus' name as his ability for doing such a miracle.[2] The disciples didn't feel that the man had the "proper authority" and had told him to stop because he wasn't one of "the chosen".

John closed his eyes as he tried to remember Jesus' exact words. "Do not stop him. Anyone who calls my name for a miracle cannot, in the next breath, say anything negative about me. Anyone who is not against us is for us."

"But, John... we're talking about Barabbas," the women cried. "Of all people... BARABBAS!"

John seemed to be speechless. "I don't think any of us can be sure. Barabbas claims to be an eye-witness to our Lord's death... and that has made an enormous impact on his life. He is a changed man. Isn't that what our Jesus would have wanted?"

I am truly shaken. I didn't expect any of the disciples

to stand up for Barabbas and his speaking in the marketplace. I'm shaken... because Barabbas claims authority declaring that his release during the Passover feast and his witness of Jesus' death had radically changed him. Oh, Lord Jesus... does Barabbas have any more authority to speak than these precious friends chosen as disciples?[3]

Oh... for every issue that is somehow clarified, many more questions come up. Please, Jesus... come back to us to help us make sense of these issues.

I tremble when I write this big question of my own... do I have any right or any authority to tell others of my joy in knowing my risen Jesus... even though I am not among "the chosen"? Is it possible... could it be... that even as a mere "tag-along", I MIGHT BE... somehow... among G*d's chosen instruments?

STOP AND REFLECT

What do you feel about the likes of Barabbas giving testimony to Jesus? What void do they fill with their witness? How and when do we question the authority of a speaker?

27. Lazarus, Mary and Martha

Dear Diary,

Earlier today, we had a quite different experience than the encounter with Barabbas; it was a pleasant surprise that broke into the monotony of our daily routine. When several of the women returned from fetching water, they could hardly contain their laughter. "Look who we met near the well!" And right behind them came our friends, Mary and Lazarus. Such joy as we greeted each other! They had come into Jerusalem for provisions, and they were hoping, yet hardly expecting, that they would be able to find us.[1]

Of course, our friends had heard the whole saga of Jesus' arrest and crucifixion... and they had been overjoyed when the grand news that Jesus was alive again rolled up across the valley and over the hill into Bethany. They cried happy tears as we described the times that Jesus had appeared among us. How they wished they could have shared that experience of being present with the living Lord! I really wonder how Jesus has chosen those to whom He has appeared after His resurrection.

Lazarus said he had no doubt that Jesus was the promised Messiah... even before he emerged from his dark grave into Jesus' embrace. He KNEW for sure that there was life after death... and he had a personal experience to prove it![2]

Mary spoke about the number of people who have found their way to their home, wanting to hear the assurance of G*d's power over their difficulties. Lazarus was laughing as he told of speaking to these visitors... they came wanting to know if G*d still had some power over blindness or lameness or leprosy... "I will never tire of telling the story! Of course, G*d has the power over such 'minor' disabilities! Look at me! G*d has the power over death!" And then our friends continue the story by talking about Jesus and all the gory and glorious events of the last several weeks.

The two of them explained that Martha has stayed back in Bethany. True to form, she was continuing to care for several visitors in their home. Martha has always displayed her gift of hospitality. Lazarus explained that they were making quite a few new friends lately; people are seeking them out to see for themselves that the story of Lazarus being brought back to life was really true. Strangers arriving at their home soon become dear friends as they have shared food and fellowship... some have stayed for longer visits before returning to their homes in other places. Mary smiled as she said, "It is good to surround ourselves with G*d's people... I feel Jesus' presence in our home when we share the experiences of our personal journeys of faith."

Lazarus and Mary (and Martha too) told us that they thought it a privilege to open their home and their lives to others; just as they had opened their home to Jesus a number of times over the years (and to us... was it really just a few short weeks ago?). They realized that people sought them out for different reasons; they were happy to share their time and hospitality with them. They admitted that they didn't fully understand all the implications, but sharing everyone's stories has become more and more important in their lives. They said it has given them pleasure and a sense of purpose.

Such dear friends!

At the same time we cherish these friends, we are disheartened and somewhat frightened that over half of the chosen disciples have given in to their frustrating restlessness; they have returned to the Galilee. They say they feel useless here in Jerusalem, and they remember Mary Magdalene's message on that day of resurrection that the Lord would go before them and meet them in Galilee. I cannot begin to describe the void in our midst.

28. Nicodemus

Dear Diary,

Well, our little group has had yet another surprise visit... this time with Nicodemus.

It was a much-needed boost for us, since so many of the disciples have returned to the Galilee, and we are left very much at odds. We will be ever grateful to Nicodemus (and, of course, to Joseph of Arimathea) for their care of Jesus' body at His hasty burial... and we have been left with many questions about Nicodemus' understanding and insight.

Our meeting had a number of twists and turns... it's taken a bit of effort to collect my thoughts enough to write all this down. I want so much to record the exact words that Nicodemus spoke.

Nicodemus has always had the reputation of being one of the wealthiest and strongest members of the Sanhedrin... I was so surprised by his humble appearance and carriage. It took a while to settle down to listen as he spoke.

Nicodemus began his story by admitting to us that he had always been proud of his studies and learning. He said he had known from an early age that the scriptures were meant to be repeated and plunged for meaning. He was fascinated by the mental stimulation of the theological depths of scriptures. "I spent my life learning, memorizing, trying to make sense of religion, learning the laws and dedicating myself to follow them diligently. I was so sure that was the path to G*d. My biggest struggle was to search out more and more information and wise commentary."

Nicodemus' demeanor changed quickly as he continued his story. "I wanted to meet Jesus,[1] mostly as a curiosity. It was all arranged under the cloak of darkness; I didn't expect it to develop into anything.

"I felt such pride when Jesus called me 'the teacher of Israel', as if He recognized and valued my vast training in

Hebrew law and tradition. Quickly then, Jesus turned my knowledge on its ear by challenging all my understanding. My head immediately began to struggle in order to defend our traditions.

"Jesus kept speaking to me... not to my ears, but to my heart. He sent my meager understanding in a completely different direction. Jesus spoke of 'heavenly things'... of true faith coming from the heart... emotional... psychological... all of which is (as it seems to me) somewhat messy.

"Then Jesus really set my mind churning... He said that a person needed to be born again in order to understand G*d's truth. When Jesus first said that, my first impulse was to scoff and ask how a grown person could be stuffed back into a mother's womb to be born a second time. But the look on Jesus' face caused me to stop and remember that that expression also means to start over and begin again. I realized that Jesus was talking about becoming a 'new creature'. My head and my heart began battling each other as never before!"

And then Nicodemus' face became so peaceful; he closed his eyes as if savoring the words as they came out of his mouth. "Jesus gave these new words to me: 'For G*d so loved the world that G*d sent the only-begotten Son into the world, that whoever believes in Him will not perish, but have eternal life. G*d did not send this Son into the world to condemn but to save the world.'[2] It gave me shivers then... and more so now, because now I KNOW... Who... that... 'only-begotten Son'... is!

"After that one encounter with Jesus, my relationship turned into affinity. I went back into my studies to discover the differences between the truth and the flimsy standing of the religious authorities.

"I'm a priest of the law; a man of centuries of tradition. I studied those ancient prophecies that promised the Messiah that G*d would send to save the people of Israel.

Those old prophecies have many times seemed so contradictory, but the more I reread them through the light of Jesus, the more they all fit."

Almost as if he were remembering for the first time as he said it, Nicodemus added: "Yes... LIGHT. THAT was a word Jesus used... seeing things in a new LIGHT. The Messiah COULD come from Bethlehem AND Galilee AND Egypt. G*d's promised Redeemer COULD take on the role the suffering servant. And the old prophecy about G*d's Mighty King riding in on the colt of a donkey... all that materialized when we saw the loud procession leading into the city of Jerusalem a couple of weeks ago. Every time I went back to the ancient scriptures for another look, I found all sorts of details set out in the ancient prophecies that have been overlooked.

"I thought I had kept my affinity for Jesus a secret... but when I spoke up that night at the trial denouncing Jesus as a false prophet, I asked (what I thought was with a cautious and guarded tone) 'Does our law judge a man before it hears him and tries to know what he is doing?'[3] At that moment my fellow members of the Sanhedrin turned on me. Oh, nothing was spoken, but there was murmuring and their eyes told me they knew the truth of my heart.

"It wasn't a surprise when Joseph (who wasn't even summoned to that mock trial) asked me to accompany him to Pilate to ask for Jesus' body late that Friday afternoon to bury it quickly.

"After the horrible crucifixion, I went out and bought a lot of spices to anoint Jesus' body. It probably took too much valuable time to do that, for it was very quickly becoming too close to sundown to properly bury the body. Again I struggled. Part of me was too aware of the prohibition of working after the Sabbath began, as well as the prohibition of touching a dead body without having the time to wash properly before the Sabbath... yet part of me was willing to risk those prohibitions in order to spread the nard that I had bought into the layers of cloth Joseph and I wrapped around the body.[4]

"I DO know that G*d has sent the Messiah to save, not only the people of Israel, but ALL people on this earth. In my life, this is the shakiest ground my feet have ever walked on... but the most grounded my heart has ever felt. I don't want to insult you, dear believers... but I will not become a follower with you. Neither am I sure if I will continue to be a member of the Sanhedrin to change the religious rules from within."

Nicodemus shook his head, and his shoulders sank as he quietly spoke, "I have two different callings... or maybe NONE at all. I'm not, hmmm... I am not... YET what I am supposed to be. But I know the truth about Jesus... and I am willing to risk the future."[5]

This story has taken so long to pour out; I am... indeed, we ALL are... filled with renewed gratitude to Nicodemus for this time we have spent together. His reassuring words have stuck with me: "I know the truth about Jesus, and I am willing to risk the future."

<u>STOP AND REFLECT</u>

Nicodemus was so proud of his head knowledge and then learned that it needed to be lived out. What knowledge about your faith has stayed in your head... and needs to reach to your heart?

---

29. Fishermen return from the Galilee

Dear Diary,

Almost as soon as they had left, the disciples have returned to us here in Jerusalem. They are very excited and newly replenished. Simon Peter and his brother Andrew, James and John, Thomas, Nathaniel, and Matthew left us less than a week ago to go back to Capernaum where it all began... where they were successful fishermen and life seemed promising.[1]

Evidently their families and fellow fishermen did not welcome them home with open arms, but rather with suspicious stares and cautious comments.

Simon Peter recounts the decision of the group to go out fishing, thinking "at least that was something familiar they could do." The group toiled with the nets throughout the night with nothing but sore muscles to show for their work. They were tired and discouraged. At the first light of dawn, the fishermen heard a voice from the shore shout out in a taunting voice: "Hey, friends, haven't you got any fish?"

Simon Peter remembered standing there in the boat... fuming... not knowing exactly how to answer that question. It was OBVIOUS that they hadn't had any luck. Those in the boat didn't recognize the guy on the beach, and being unfamiliar to them, they thought he probably didn't know the first thing about fishing. But the guy was persistent and told them to lower their nets on the OTHER side of the boat!

The fishermen were SO tired and frustrated that they didn't have the strength to complain about the folly: "Yeah, right! One side or the other!"

All seven of the disciples were adding a little bit to the story at this point. They recalled thinking that they were total failures... even their fishing expedition was a bust. And that voice was mocking them about their own professional ability. They felt "out to sea" in so many different ways.

"Trust me! Cast down your nets into the deeper water on the other side. There's a larger haul just waiting for you!"

The disciples did as the voice suggested, not so much to follow those directions, but rather to prove it wrong! Suddenly, the problem changed! Instead of empty nets, the nets were SO FULL of fish that they were breaking under the strain of too heavy a load.

Simon Peter was the first to recognize that it was our Lord who was standing on the beach... and he forgot his shame about meeting Jesus face to face. He jumped overboard, swimming to shore to get there more quickly (and, as the others recalled, he had left ALL the work of those over-filled nets to the others!)

Before long, Jesus and the seven disciples were sharing breakfast on the beach. Surrounding Jesus, they were stuffed with fish and bread, as well as filled with the presence of our risen Lord. As the little group recalled this meal with us, they also remembered another time that Jesus had used fish and bread to feed hungry stomachs and souls...

Almost as if these dear friends had run out of energy as they finished their story, the room became very quiet... but NO!... it was a SACRED SILENCE... their faces were vibrant and joyful! There was a new reflection shining from each disciple.

Long ago, Jesus called them saying that He would make them fishers... not just of fish from the sea, but fishers of PEOPLE. Back then, they had given little thought to the implications of that. Now... they all realize that they are, somehow, looking to brand new professions.

STOP AND REFLECT

Do you remember a time of discouragement when God "interfered?"

---

30. Peter tells his story "Do you love me?"

Dear Diary,

    I have to admit that of all the chosen disciples, Simon Peter is my favorite. (Although not among the twelve "chosen", Mary Magdalene ranks right up there in my estimation!). Simon Peter was never afraid to ask questions, or to take chances, or to risk sounding dumb. He always spoke up... sometimes out of turn and many times, way too soon. He was ambitious, curious, and sometimes unclear. We have all heard about the time that Simon Peter actually walked on top of the water[1] while looking straight at Jesus (and much later, Simon Peter laughed when he remembered his panic when Jesus had to pluck him out of the deep waves!) At times he was brave and protective (I remember him cutting off the guard's ear in the garden)... and other times he was afraid and chose his own safety. It seems that Peter has never given up trying... working... and seeking to be true to the person that Jesus saw him to be. This assures me that our G*d can and will use anybody for the building of G*d's kingdom.

    It almost destroyed Simon Peter that Jesus was correct in predicting that he would deny knowing Him. That shame caused him such fear of a future face-to-face meeting with Jesus. How could Jesus POSSIBLY forgive him for denying Him? Of course, Simon Peter's shame hits us all... because he had to be there in the courtyard to face the accusers. The rest of us, on the other hand, had scattered into the darkness in our fear of the authorities. Did Jesus also know that we would all vanish into the night completely abandoning Him? Are we any less guilty of denying our love for Jesus than Simon Peter? Hmmm... did Jesus somehow point His predicting finger at ALL of us during that Passover meal?

    After the fishermen enjoyed breakfast with Jesus on the beach at the Galilee, they said that Jesus approached

Simon Peter... and he had no idea what to expect. Jesus addressed him only as "Simon"... and he expected some accusation. As he spoke to us, he became very emotional.[2] "Jesus first addressed me as 'Simon, son of John' and my heart sank. Then Jesus asked me if I loved Him. Of course, I responded that YES, I loved Him! I needed so desperately for Him to know that! Jesus MUST have known it! Jesus who knows everything about us... WHY did He have to ask? Then Jesus asked me that same question THREE TIMES... and I was so dismayed that He had to ask more than once. But then, when He asked the THIRD time, I hesitated... not because I didn't love Him, but because I realized that Jesus was giving me the gracious opportunity to repent of denying Him those three times!"

Jesus went on to tell him to feed His lambs... and care for His sheep. (I think that is a strange assignment for a fisherman, but then again, we can be sure that Jesus knows what He is talking about.)

Simon Peter continued saying that he was filled with pride that Jesus trusted him so. Then, his head fell to his chest as he admitted, "Well... right away, I BLEW IT... once again. No sooner had Jesus forgiven me that I dared ask about the one who had betrayed Him.[3] I confess that I let my arrogance resurface... and I guess I wanted to believe that my offense of denial was less than Judas' sin of betraying Him. It wasn't the first time that my Jesus rebuked me for my self-pride."

We watched as our friend fought tears while trying to find his thoughts and words. He recalled the time when Jesus renamed him "Peter"[4]... a rock upon which the church (whatever a church is) would be built. Simon's brow furrowed as he remembered that, in that same conversation, Jesus also called him "Satan"[5] for some impetuous remark he had made... adding that Simon could easily become a different type of rock... that is, a STUMBLING STONE!

With all the inner strength he could muster, our dear friend raised his head and squared his shoulders as he declared: "I... WILL... BE... THE... ROCK! I... WILL... BE... PETER!"[6]

Oh Lord Jesus, help each of us find the needed strength and the courage and the humility to discover who and what You want us to be!

STOP AND REFLECT

When in your life have you experienced total (and surprising) forgiveness? What changed?

---

31. Meeting Jesus' younger brother, James

Dear Diary,

When the disciples returned from the Galilee, we were delighted to see that Jesus' younger brother, James[1], had accompanied them. James had been here in Jerusalem with his mother, Mary, for the Passover commemoration. They were witnesses to the horrible events of Jesus' death, and they celebrated Jesus' resurrection with us before returning to Nazareth.

It was such FUN to hear James tell stories about Jesus... Although the chosen disciples had stories of their own during the time they traveled with Jesus, somehow we had never felt the need to ask Jesus about His own childhood and youth. We giggled as we listened... all the while seeing our Lord in a new light...

We all settled in for an evening of stories that none of us had ever heard. James reminisced about growing up with "Mr. Perfect" as his big brother. He said that Jesus was never smug or arrogant, but everything was easy for Him. Jesus knew ALL the answers almost before the questions were asked... and always answered with a slight smile. Playing games was frustrating... Jesus always knew where the other kids were hiding... and no one could keep a secret around Him. At school, Jesus tackled all the lessons as if He were born with the knowledge. The synagogue leaders were so very impressed with Jesus' easy understanding of the ancient scriptures that were being studied. James recalled a time when Jesus cuddled an injured bird, whispered into its ears and it flew away, singing. Although neither of their parents ever said it, many neighbors wanted to know of James: "why can't you be more like your older brother?"

James admitted that the only time he was jealous of Jesus was the time that He got to go with Mary and Joseph to Jerusalem.[2] James had so wanted to go, but was "too young" and had to stay at home with his grandmother, Sabba Anne. James remembered that the three didn't return with the rest of the group that had traveled together... there was a lot of "hush-hush" explanation with their Sabba about what had occurred, but the younger members of the family got only snippets of explanation and never really knew why they were detained in Jerusalem.

James also told us about a neighborhood wedding feast that the whole family was attending.[3] James remembered there was some "misunderstanding" about the wine needed to serve to the guests. James saw Mary drag Jesus away, forcing Him to perform a wine-producing miracle for their friends so as to avoid embarrassment. Afterwards, Jesus melted into the background, not wanting ANY attention, and no longer seemed to enjoy the feast. James said, as he looked back... that he should have connected the dots about Jesus' ability and identity... but "come on, he was my big brother!"

Then... later... there was that episode at the synagogue in Nazareth.[4] Mary had urged James and the other three brothers (Joseph, Simon and Judas) to attend this particular Sabbath gathering with her because she was afraid for Jesus and wanted them to bring Him back before anything bad happened to Him. James admitted that he tried to make some excuse... after all, Jesus was a grown man and should have been able to take care of Himself... but their mother was really distressed. On that occasion, as was His custom, Jesus stood to read the scripture of the day... and then had the audacity to proclaim that the scripture was being fulfilled in the eyes of all who gathered there at that time. That "news" was not well-received by the congregation. "I agreed with the murmurs of the crowd... yes! That is my brother... yes! He's the home-town boy, just the son of Joseph the carpenter." The crowd was angry, but Jesus seemed to quietly slip through to safety. Again, James admitted that he and his brothers should have understood better what was happening in their family. It was much later that James realized that Mary knew the truth... Mary KNEW that Jesus deserved honor even in their hometown, but had kept it all in her heart.

James confessed that he was miffed when Jesus didn't settle down with a wife and family as all young men were expected to do... and then suddenly up and left the carpentry business that He and their father had previously developed. During the three years that Jesus traveled around with His entourage, James considered his brother's travels merely as a fun junket with a group of light-hearted friends, shirking real work.

Yes, James assured us... he had heard all about that "miracle man" teaching and healing all over the area but did not believe it all.[5] "He was, after all, my flesh and blood brother." James and the other brothers never hid their skepticism... they felt dismissed as blood family when Jesus said publicly that He embraced other "believers" over His own family.[6] At one point, James and his brothers even goaded Jesus to go on to Judea, daring Him to show off His abilities there (even knowing that it would be dangerous).[7]

James got a bit nervous when he spoke about meeting us when he had accompanied Mary to celebrate the Passover commemoration with Jesus. He said he didn't want to come... he really wanted to celebrate the Passover with his own family, not with a group of vagabonds. But Mary had insisted, and being a good son, he consented. "I was so skeptical of this group... of my own brother... of the danger the authorities thought He presented. I figured Jesus was getting Himself into trouble, but I never imagined the authorities would go to such horrible lengths to settle 'the problem'. The Romans and the Pharisees gave such credence to Jesus... I was amazed that they believed all that stuff that my brother was saying. It surprised me... and honestly confused me to witness the... the... extent of all the events that led to my brother's death."

James was present at the crucifixion... he said he was more distressed for his mother who had to watch it all than he was for himself. "I felt so very numb! My big brother was being unfairly crucified... CRUCIFIED like a CRIMINAL! My brother may have been somewhat irresponsible in some of the things He was saying and doing, but He was NOT a criminal! I'm not sure how He did it all, but He had helped lots of people and had done a lot of good things. He was a GOOD MAN. He was a GOOD BIG BROTHER! I was in such shock that I wasn't feeling anything. And I was really confused when Jesus gave responsibility for our mother to John. NOTHING was making sense!"

James recalled feeling like he was "a fly on the wall" as he watched his mother and our group react in the hours after Jesus' death. Nothing seemed real... everyone was going through the motions.

On that first day of the week, James wasn't surprised when he woke up from a fitful sleep to find that his mother had already left with the other Marys to see if they could better attend Jesus' buried body. As the news of Jesus' resurrection began reverberating through Jerusalem and its environs, James remembers being very confused and still very skeptical... until he saw the look of quiet peace radiating from his mother's eyes. She KNEW all this would work out just the way Jesus had said. Of course, she was deeply hurt that her son had to suffer so... but she was quietly at peace, even as the others in the group loudly celebrated the news of that day. "As much as anything else, it was that look of peaceful assurance that made me believe in Jesus as Lord and Savior. Imagine... I am one of only a handful of people on this earth who can say that we knew Jesus all our lives when He was simply a boy... a young man... our big brother... at least we THOUGHT we knew the man Jesus was to become."

James and his mother had returned to Nazareth shortly after the resurrection. James told us of the conversations he and his mother had as they traveled home. For the first time, James heard many things that Mary had long kept in her heart. James heard the full story of his mother's pregnancy while she and his father were still engaged. Mary tried to put into words the appearance of an angel announcing the improbable news about the baby she was carrying, and then, about the way her beloved Joseph was led to accept this amazing pregnancy. Mary told him all that had happened in their hometown of Nazareth, explaining the reason there has always been some bit of gossip about Joseph's family. He learned about the need to travel to Bethlehem and the humble circumstances of Jesus' birth... in a STABLE, no less. And then narrowly escaping to Egypt, carrying some very expensive gifts with them, before being able to return to Nazareth and pick up the pieces of a "normal" family. James was amazed to hear all that family history for the first time... and he admitted that, maybe, his understanding of his brother would have been different had he known.

After all this poured out... James took a deep breath and quietly said, "I have seen Him.[7] When Jesus came to me, I thought it was a dream... then He put His hands firmly on my shoulders. He told me that it had been a privilege to act as my older brother and that He had no doubt that I would go on to do great things. Then He hugged me before leaving. It all happened too fast... there were so many things I would have liked to talk about, but then again, by that point... He knew that I believed in Him and nothing more needed to be said between us."

It was strange to hear James speaking... this son of Mary and Joseph... growing up thinking that he and Jesus were brothers... and only after Jesus' death and resurrection, did he come to the realization that they were really HALF-brothers.

As I watched James relate this whole story with us, I was amazed that he has now humbled himself to accept that his older brother was exactly who He said He was. In fact, of all the people who had to swallow their pride, I believe James had to swallow the most. I can't imagine how many times James loudly scoffed at Jesus' followers who were so "naive" as to think that Jesus was the promised Messiah. And now that the resurrection has vindicated Jesus' claims, James has had to admit he'd been wrong all those years.

It was then that the disciples who had traveled to the Galilee added that James had sought them out while they were in that area. No one is quite sure of what this all means, but James felt drawn to return here to Jerusalem with them.[8,9]

Even though I don't fully understand all that is happening either... I'm beginning to feel deeply that the plan and purpose of everything will be revealed at the proper time. But I STILL wish I could make sense of this all and understand it all... even just a little bit better.

STOP AND REFLECT

Again, has your imagination been inspired to create the "back story" of someone barely mentioned in scripture?

32. On prayer

Dear Diary,

As we go through the motions of living, waiting, hoping, eating, waiting, sleeping, waiting, living, leaving only when we absolutely need to go out into the city... we are trying very hard to continue to celebrate the joy of our resurrected Jesus. It seemed easier when He appeared among us, giving us assurance. It's SO difficult to remain here when we have little direction or real purpose. The disciples who returned from the Galilee have been instrumental in helping us remain united... although our focus seems so fuzzy.

As we worship together, we sing and we pray. Our traditional songs of David[1] have such a wide range of emotions and cover so many different situations; they are joyful and praising... they are calming and encouraging... they are sometimes angry and even vindictive... all honestly reflecting such a wide range of emotions. There are some talented singers among us who are composing new songs for us to sing!

But it's our practice of prayer that is proving to be a greater challenge. The men are well-versed in the traditional ritual prayers, and they take turns leading us. Our biggest comfort is that, by necessity, we are inside in this place... so we can follow part of the advice that Jesus gave us, saying that we should not stand on street corners like Pharisees who want to be seen. This place is not exactly a "QUIET corner", and we aren't praying only to attract public attention. Oh, my heart cries out for the attention of our great G*d... but in these days, that seems hard to feel. Am I the only one who feels that those ancient Hebrew prayers don't always "fit" anymore? Is it possible that we are supposed to be "composing" new prayers as well as new songs?

Many of us remember Jesus' teaching about prayer, promising that "WHATEVER was asked for in prayer would be given to us".[2] Right now, I don't think any of us knows WHAT to ask for. I continue to pray for Jesus to appear with us again, so we can ask Him how to pray better. I remember seeing Jesus go off by Himself during the night to pray and He always seemed refreshed in the morning even though He hadn't slept. For me, our prayers seem more frustrating than refreshing. I'm pretty sure this isn't what is supposed to happen.

We remember and often repeat the prayer that Jesus gave us so long ago:[3] "Our Father... who art in heaven, hallowed be thy name. Thy kingdom come, thy will be done on earth as it is in heaven. Give us this day our daily bread, and forgive us our debts, as we forgive our debtors. And lead us not into temptation, but deliver us from evil. So be it." When Jesus taught these WORDS, He said to the disciples: "This is the WAY you are to pray." I'm starting to wonder if this pattern is the complete "WAY"... if it's an END in itself... or just the beginning to something else. (I'm also continuing to wonder if maybe I wonder about too many things.)

John is the deepest soul among us and certainly the most articulate. In a time of quiet, it was obvious that he wanted to speak, but was hesitant and was choosing his words very carefully. "I do believe that we are mistakenly focused on the WORDS that we are praying. I think that our preoccupation about the words is getting in the way of our real prayers." Boy! THAT caught MY attention... as it did of all of us gathered there.

John went on to propose that we enter into a time of prayer without words... simply breathing deeply and allowing the beat of our hearts to guide us. We all got comfortable and settled into a time of purposeful quiet. And it worked... for just a couple of minutes... until little noises of restlessness began to interrupt.

There were some sighs of frustration as John urged us to try again, reminding us that the psalmist sang for us "to be still and know that our G*d is our G*d."[4]

On our next tries, we endured a little bit longer... but it's really HARD to be quiet and still with so many people and so many thoughts and questions in our minds and hearts demanding to be set free! It feels strange for each of us to pray our own thoughts in silence... we are so accustomed to being LED in our prayers. Hmmm.

John in particular, but others say such beautiful things when they lead us. I wish I could write their words down. John stopped me once when I started writing, saying: "Pray YOUR OWN WORDS." But MY words don't sound half as holy as his. Will G*d hear ME?

John again spoke about his growing understanding that our prayers needed to include times for LISTENING as well as times for speaking. Oh, but... WHAT are we supposed to listen for?

John closed his eyes and sighed deeply before quietly saying: "I'm afraid that the peace we are all yearning won't be found in our times of quiet. Even our lack of spoken prayers and praises is not necessarily G*d's peace. I believe that the quiet listening we need to pursue will not always be assuring, but rather may become RISKY. I believe that our faithful listening will ultimately lead us from our safe existence into some form of action."[5]

Oh dear... THAT isn't quite what I think I want to hear... or even think about. Maybe it would simply be easier to be satisfied with the words of the ancient rituals. Oh, sweet Jesus... come back to us soon! There is so much we don't understand!

STOP AND REFLECT

Prayer is a vitally important part of our faithful lives. May your time spent in prayer be as fruitful and refreshing as it was for Jesus and His followers. Here are some suggestions:

START WITH JESUS
There's a reason Jesus gave us a model to begin our prayers. Pray it slowly!

ADVICE OF A CHILD
All you need to do is connect your heart and your mouth and start talking. Just talk to God as if God were sitting right next to you. Get real. Be honest.

FIND YOUR OWN WAY
Your own prayers are the best and are perfect. Talk with others about their prayer life, then experiment to find what prayer form "works" for you. Read others' prayers, then use your own words (and not always repeat those "pretty" words spoken by someone else).

BREATHE!
At the tiny gaps in your day (at a red light, in line at the store), simply breathe deeply and relax in God's love.

BREATH PRAYER
If you must pray in those gaps… on in-breath, say a name you have for God; on out-breath, say your prayer in a few words. Repeat it.

READ A PSALM

ACTS
ADORATION: Tell God of your love.
CONFESSION: Let it out (be specific), then let it go.
THANKSGIVING: Be specific, especially for the little things.
SUPPLICATION: Say what's on your heart.

YOUR "HANDY" GUIDE
<u>Thumb</u>
Pray for those who are closest to you.
<u>Index (the pointer)</u>
Pray for those who are far away.
<u>Middle (tallest)</u>
Pray for ALL leaders.
<u>Ring (weakest)</u>
Pray for those in need and in despair.
<u>Little</u>
Pray for yourself.
<u>Palm</u>
Give thanks that you are in the palm of God's hand.

If we are to pray "at all times," we must admit that really short, honest prayers offered at random are still valid. Rather than tidy and eloquent wording, we should allow some run-on sentences and messy thoughts when the situations are confusing. (Our whole lives may seem to be lived as a big, giant, messy prayer.) We recognize that laughter and tears are forms of prayer. At times, we depend on the words that others write. Sometimes we have to sit with ourselves and God in silence. And from time to time, we will live out the prayer in our actions. So be it. **Amen**

33. Saturday evening—the Sabbath has ended; (Jesus lifted into Heaven)

Dear Diary,

I suppose today's is the most astonishing entry since our Lord's resurrection some six weeks ago. I'm running out of words to express the sense of "unbelievable."

During each of the number of times that Jesus has appeared in our presence over these last weeks, we have asked Him what He wanted us to do. He never answered our questions directly... He hinted that we were to wait for further instructions, saying a couple of times that "the Comforter" would come to guide us in our future endeavors.

I wondered what on earth "the Comforter" could possibly be... it sounds more like a warm blanket than a leader. Jesus also said that "the Spirit" would guide us... none of us is sure what to expect. But I will trust Jesus with my being, even as I am impatient to find out who is coming to lead us.

As I wonder what our new leader will look like, I hope we will recognize him when he comes to us. I worry that we won't know who it is. Is there any possibility that our new leader will be "SHE"? Jesus used the word "spirit." I almost don't dare to think that our new leader might be something other than a human... I remember feeling the sense of WIND when Jesus blew some sort of spirit into us... or maybe a FIRE, like the flames that guided Moses and the ancient Israelites... or perhaps some great WATERFALL in this desert land. Jesus often spoke of LIVING WATER that could quench our great thirst for... for... I don't even know what we really crave and need from our Jesus. Whenever someone new arrives, we all wonder: "is THIS our new leader? Is THIS the one whom G*d is now sending?"

There have been a lot of bumps in the road, but our group has managed to stay pretty much together, which is a miracle in itself. We have learned so much about each other as we share the stories of our lives. In addition to all the daily chores, we sit and remember the stories and the things that happened to us and around us as we traveled with Jesus during those many months and years. SO MUCH has happened! HOW will all this be remembered and passed along to others? Mark still talks about writing all this down; he is starting to write notes here and there, but admits that he doesn't know where to start or how he might end up putting all these little pieces of notes into some sort of proper order.

There seems to be less bickering in our group now... like we are starting to all stand shoulder to shoulder looking in the SAME direction, rather than each person looking out for his or her own best interests.

Anyway, I digress. Last Thursday, Jesus again appeared to us. Instead of staying safely inside this closed home, He urged us to follow Him out into the streets and across the valley. That idea terrified us; if it were anyone else, we certainly would not have obeyed. As we all headed out... all of us together for the first time in weeks... Jesus talked about this "Holy Spirit" that would baptize us with some kind of spirit, just as John had baptized with water. I wanted so to ask lots of questions, but Jesus was walking so fast and carried Himself with such an air of authority that I didn't want to spoil the ambiance with what seemed like my silly questions.

We were all the way out on the Mount of Olives,[1] and someone in the group dared to ask if this were the time that He was going to restore the kingdom to the people of Israel. Jesus stopped short and quickly declared that it wasn't for any of us to know the exact time that His Father had planned for such a deliverance. He repeated that "the Holy Spirit" would come to us and give us power. "Give US power??" "Give us POWER!?!?" "What KIND of power?" My heart skipped a beat and my mind puzzled: "Power for WHAT???" I almost missed the next part of what Jesus said: "You shall be My witnesses in Jerusalem; and in all of Judea and Samaria; and even to the remotest parts of the earth."

I nearly fainted right out there. I could understand the Jerusalem part... that's already happening some. I could even imagine parts of Judea... but Samaria and the remotest parts of the earth??? How could our little group of disciples and followers, even with the power that Jesus promised... how could we be witnesses all over the world???

It seems impossible! As soon as the word "impossible" crosses my mind, I remember the time long ago now, when Jesus had told a story, finishing by saying, "With men all this is impossible, but with G*d all things are possible."

"With G*d, all things are possible."[2]

Jesus led us right up to the Mount of Olives. I think we all wanted to grab Jesus and get some more details about what He meant. But all of a sudden, He was being lifted up as if He were standing on a cloud. As He floated up, He commanded us to go and teach and baptize, in the name of the Father, the Son, and the Holy Spirit.[3] I had NEVER heard THAT combination before... but He was floating up and out of our sight as He spoke, so there was no opportunity to question.

Just before He rose up so far that He disappeared from our sight, He whispered into our hearts: "I am with you always, even to the end of the age..." And then... then... and then He was... gone.

Jesus has disappeared before. In the several times He has come into our presence since that great Sunday morning of His resurrection, He has somehow "melted" from our sight... but this seemed different. Oh, my Lord... I don't think He is coming back this time...

Strange. I am not afraid. I am saddened, yet strangely excited. I can't quite pinpoint exactly WHAT I'm feeling. It's an exciting and scary combination of expectation and, yet ... somewhat of a burden. What does all this mean?

I can't even fathom!

We all stood there for a long time... no one spoke, no one moved. I really don't know how long we stood out there, when a passer-by asked us why we were all staring at the sky. The REALLY weird thing was that these people were dressed strangely, as if their clothes were made out of bright puffy clouds. Whew! Jesus has really done a number on us!!4

Even as I write this, I am aware that this episode elicits more questions than it clarifies about what has happened. Even as I put these words on paper, there's a certain amount of unrealistic dreaminess. It's hard to express what is real and what isn't.

We kept the Sabbath today... but I really look forward to tomorrow. We continue to gather to worship together on the mornings of the first day of the week as well as observing the Sabbath. This new gathering has become so meaningful... there are new songs and new prayers, and this gathering has become so very special as we share bread outside of our regular meal times. Hmmm... are we still Jewish???

STOP AND REFLECT

When have you experienced the truth that "all things are possible!"? Reflect on Jesus' promise to YOU: "I will be with you always."

34. Choosing Matthias

Dear Diary,

When Nicodemus visited us, he opened our eyes to many of the ancient prophecies whose meanings about the promised Messiah seemed ambiguous and contradictory until Jesus fulfilled them ALL. After that visit, Luke and John and Peter have delved more deeply into the ancient scriptures.

In their studies they even found the prophecy that the Messiah would be betrayed by a friend and that that former companion would die in a horrible way.[1] Could it be that Judas was DESTINED by G*d to his role as betrayer? Could it possibly be that it wasn't Judas' personal choice when he set into action all the events of that terrible (and ultimately, WONDERFUL) several days way back then??

They also found basis in David's writings that a replacement to Judas would be chosen.[2] Peter stood and read: "May another be chosen to take that disciple's place in the leadership."[3]

It was determined that the man should be among those who had been with Jesus since the beginning of His ministry and who had been a witness to His death and resurrection. Among us, two men fit that description: Barsabbas (whom we nicknamed "Justus") and Matthias. These two have been an integral part of our group for as long as I have been with them. For a long time, I honestly thought that they were among "the chosen twelve". Both Barsabbas and Matthias told stories about their experiences when, quite a while ago, Jesus had sent SEVENTY of the disciples and other "tag-alongs" to go out to heal the sick and preach the good news of the Kingdom of G*d.[4]

I couldn't imagine how this group could possibly decide between these two righteous and capable followers. Maybe BOTH of them could replace Judas... Is twelve such a magic number? What's wrong with thirteen?

We prayed together for a long time... that our G*d would show us which man G*d would choose to take a more active part in the ministry. All this seems so confusing! Here we were, trying to decide who would take Judas' place... yet at the same time, I'm not sure any of us knows for sure WHY any replacement will be needed. Here I go wondering again... am I the only one whose logical head and trusting heart are at odds?

It was then decided to draw lots to determine which man to choose.[5] LOTS! It has always seemed to me that drawing sticks is a flimsy way to decide important matters. My brothers used to decide things that way... and I always thought that they had rigged the size of the sticks to serve their own desires. Hmmm. But here we were... in a sense, putting sticks into our G*d's hands to choose between Barsabbas and Matthias.

Well, the lot fell to Matthias. The choice being made, there was no sense of victory; we had to believe that our G*d had spoken. Matthias seemed strangely overwhelmed. I couldn't tell from Barsabbas' face whether he felt relief or disappointment.

Even with all the confusion in my soul, I think I'm still glad that I somehow made the choice to be a "tag-along" with Jesus... and now with this group. I really hope this "gamble" will be worth it!

STOP AND REFLECT

How does God "interfere" in our options and choices? What are the "odds" that God can impact our "gambling"?

---

35. After the Sabbath... everything in shambles

Dear Diary,

Just when we thought the waiting was difficult, it has become insupportable!

It has been a very difficult week here as we wait... as we wait FOR... something to happen... someone to come. In this uncertain time, I so want to remember that there should be a certain amount of HOPE in our waiting, but it's getting harder and harder to remain hopeful.

Oh dear. Have we sung "hallelujah" too many times? What is happening to our "resurrection feeling" of new life and awesome possibilities? Is it possible to be JOYFUL at the same time we seem so distressed?

In one of my last entries, I noted that we had somehow managed to stay together. I must have doomed us by that statement, for lately, our time together has been less than encouraging. I am more convinced than ever that we need to pray for one another... not for any specific need, but right now our common prayers are the only thing that unite us.

The other day, we just stared at each other; there was a profound silence as we tried to think of what to DO. How long will we wait? How will we live? Who will continue to provide for us? Our dear friends here have been extremely generous to help provide for our needs, including this house where we are staying. Obviously, we can't stay here in Jerusalem. We don't have any way to earn a living if we don't return to our homes and professions. Where is our Jesus now that we really need Him? After all, He PROMISED to be WITH us always!!

One voice spoke up and articulated our worst fear: "He's gone... FOREVER! This is the end of Jesus, you know."

From way over in the corner came the sobs of one whose grief was bubbling to the surface... a grief that had been interrupted nearly fifty days ago by that astounding announcement telling us that grieving for the LIVING wasn't necessary. And now the grief is coming back. It really is... ALL OVER! A stronger disciple next to that person wrapped his arms around the sobbing body and whispered, "Don't cry. He isn't with us, but He's still alive... there's no reason to grieve or to be afraid." And then THAT disciple also broke down as the aching and longing in his heart overcame the words of his mouth. And the sobs spread and grew and continued for a long time... until there were no more tears... and quiet emotional exhaustion filled the room.

Someone by the door lowered the bar to lock us in. It wasn't an act of obedience to Jesus' instructions to stay in this place, but an act of fear of what peril lurked in the streets for those of us who had formerly been the disciples of Jesus of Nazareth. One tried to escape the terrifying fears of the room and was held back by several others: "You can't leave, it's worse out there than it is in here."

There are no answers available as some here cry out in anguish, "WHAT are we going to DO?" "Why are we enduring this hopeless situation?" "WHY are we staying here?"

All of us who have remained here are SOOO different. Our only common bond had been Jesus. Now that He is forever gone, there seem to be no ties to keep us together... no reason for being a group. So, for a while, each of us has retreated into our private world of hurt and fear and uncertainty. This place is CROWDED with lonely people! The members of this group who had previously shared so much with each other... now each is desperately trying to hold things together inside themselves.

Tempers have flared as they will with any group confined to close quarters. After an angry episode with a group of people on THIS side of the house, one brother moved to the OTHER side, only to move back again when the others were no friendlier.

The anguish has just mounted! One sister stood right here in the middle of the room and shouted, "I can't stand it! I hate this! I hate G*d. I hate myself! There is absolutely no reason for living! I just want to DIE!"

Over the course of the last several days, tensions have flared and then settled, arguments raged and then subsided. One brother remembered something that Jesus had said and reminded the rest of the group that He would not leave us alone. He was immediately shot down: "Can't you get it through your head that Jesus isn't here anymore... and what He started is all over!?!?"

Then another brother ventured to bring up one of the stories that Jesus had told us about His words being like seeds that were sown in different soils. He was immediately interrupted: "Stop talking about Jesus! It hurts me to think about Him and to hear about Him. I think it'll be better if we forget Him and figure out a way to get on with our lives."

But from the other side of the room, a small voice admitted that hearing those stories about Jesus made her feel less afraid. A few others agreed.

The stories and the anecdotes tentatively started to flow:

"Do you remember that time that Jesus stood up to the Pharisees? I felt such pride to be with Him then. I wish I had the wisdom to answer all those questions about the law."

"Does anyone remember exactly what Jesus said that day when He raised His friend, Lazarus? It started out something like 'I am the resurrection and the life, and...' What was the end of that?" And someone else excitedly proclaimed "I will NEVER forget that day as long as I live. Jesus' words were carved into my soul, but I had forgotten them until just now. He said, 'I am the resurrection and the life. Those who believe in Me, though they be dead, yet shall they live, and whoever lives and believes in Me shall never die.'¹ That day I felt like I wanted to repeat those words to everyone that I met..." Then he very hesitantly admitted: "You know, I would still like to tell people about Jesus."

Another sister piped up: "Jesus taught us a song one day... and she began to hum. "Oh, I remember that," answered another, singing: 'Seek ye first the kingdom of G*d, and his righteousness... da da da da'". And someone else picked it right up: "'And all these things shall be given unto you.'[2] Let's sing it together!" And as we were singing, we relaxed, and smiles returned to our faces.

Right in the middle, a sister stood up and said, "I wanted to run away from here a couple of days ago, and I hated you when you forced me to stay. Now I'm glad I'm here. I feel good when I'm with all of you. I somehow feel hopeful and strong. Thank you for being my friends." And she hugged the person next to her. Incredibly others stood and hugged each other. And there was a quiet hum in the room as we began to really talk with each other again, as we comforted each other, dried each other's tears, confessed our fears and doubts to each other and realized that EVERYONE had the same fears and doubts. There was a burst of laughter in the far corner of the room.

The wooden windows were opened for the first time in more than a week, and the fresh breeze and bright sunlight exploded into the room.

With the new energy came the renewed realization that we are indeed ALIVE ... and HUNGRY! "I could eat a whole cow by myself," exclaimed one brother. But one of the women added, "Well, curb your appetite, because all we have is some bread, some dried fish and half a bottle of wine." The initial shock of having no food gave way to the memory of several meals shared with Jesus, meals with similar ingredients... and we realized almost all at the same time that we really had plenty. Our whole group joyfully partook of a sumptuous meal together.

Afterwards, as we relaxed, someone said, "This may sound strange, but I feel very close to Jesus because I feel very close to all of you. I can't explain it... but I think you all feel the same way, don't you?"

Another voice started out hesitantly: "I don't know quite how to say this... I have never said this to anyone before... but I... love you. I love you all. I don't understand it, but I feel such a love for you and for the whole world. I want to go out and tell everyone." Let's go out and share our news. John (who is older and wiser) said, "We too want to go out and tell all the people, but I don't think that we're ready. I believe that Jesus had something else in mind when He told us to wait for a special gift from our G*d. Jesus never lied to us before. Even though we don't know what that gift might be... I think that we should be together here... and wait."

These are the problems and the hopes that are ours.[3] It's so hard to hold fast to the idea that all things are possible with our G*d. At times, I feel like we are moving ahead... and at the same time, I fear that we are quickly heading toward the edge of a high cliff. And beyond that... WHAT? Will there be some form of solid ground... or will we incredibly learn how to fly? We continue to hold each other in prayer.

STOP AND REFLECT

It has been said that life looks bleakest just before something important is about to happen. How does this entry make you feel about this group of Jesus' followers? Does this resonate with anything happening to you?

36. Several days after the day of Pentecost

Dear Diary,

These last couple of days have been SO significant! I feel at a complete loss as I try to put these events into words, but I want to try to record some of this grand and wonderful jumble because I want to remember the details.

Indeed, the most incredible, unbelievable, marvelous, miraculous thing has happened. Oh, I must slow down before I get waaaaay ahead of myself. Just a couple of days ago, I spoke of the difficulties that we all were having waiting here as Jesus told us to. It seemed that we didn't have a prayer of staying united, but our G*d had other ideas... somehow, we managed to find some hope and encouragement and strength.

The next day after my last entry was the first day of the week. We stayed inside, as usual, where we felt some modicum of safety. Although the grand Feast of Weeks was happening all around us in Jerusalem, we were hesitant to go outside without Jesus heading up our parade. There were thousands of visitors from all over the world in the city... all following the mandate to worship in the Temple during these special feast days.[1] Jews were coming from as far away as Macedonia, Mesopotamia, Egypt and Libya. All were coming to celebrate this Pentecost feast of the harvest, held fifty days after the Feast of Unleavened Bread. We probably would have blended in with so many strangers, but it seemed safer to hang in together than wander around in the streets.

It was rather early on that Sunday morning, and we were just beginning to get organized for the day. We've gotten into the habit of worshiping together early on the first day of the week in celebration of the day that Jesus rose from the dead. But we hadn't yet started our worship time together. I have often remarked how quiet our meeting time is, even when so many of us are in this same place... I count that peacefulness as a blessing we share. Suddenly, it WASN'T quiet at all![2] There was a noise like rushing wind as during a violent storm... and it was INSIDE our house. The strange thing was that it didn't shake the windows and walls, like a real wind. Oh, it was real all right, and it shook the very foundations of our souls!!! It was so sudden and so fierce that we shut our eyes tight and drew up our arms and shoulders as some sort of self-protection. There was no way to look around to see what the cause might be.

With that raging wind came the... the... (gosh, I don't know what to call it!)... the PRESENCE that filled every single space in that large room... every bit of space both inside us and around us.

When I could open my eyes, the first thing I saw was fire... FIRE everywhere! But strangely, it didn't scare me. There was a gentle explosion that left little pieces of flame, like little tongues of fire all around us... and they seemed to be resting on the tops of the heads of each of the disciples and friends gathered in the room.

Almost before it registered in my mind that there was fire in the room, I felt another... another... another... (my goodness, again, I can't think of a good word to describe it). I guess I would have to say that I felt another PRESENCE inside me. I had felt it before when Jesus appeared to us after His resurrection and breathed on us (INTO us, really). He had called it the "Holy Spirit". This time, I felt that I would burst open again, with a feeling that I have never experienced before, a feeling of... of... of intense love and elation and peace and empowerment and courage and knowledge and insight and faith and strength and excitement and a strange restlessness... ALL these wrapped into one unbelievable wave sweeping over me and through me. From the reactions around me, it was the same with each one in that place. Whew!!!

As quickly as the noise filled the room, it stopped. The noise stopped but the feeling remained!!

We all looked at each other and watched the little flames consume themselves and disappear into our hearts. I know this sounds really, really strange as I write this... but it gets even stranger!!! The room felt THICK with something other than just air... the fire was replaced with a sense of peace... and strength... and conviction... and what I can only call "holy fear". Tears spilled from our eyes into our throats gushing with laughter.

We instantly knew that this was it, this... this... this "Holy Spirit" was the comforter, the gift that Jesus had told us we should wait for. My meager words cannot do justice to this... this feeling... this knowledge... this presence... this infilling... this promise being fulfilled in our hearts and souls!

This all seems to be so jumbled as I try to write down these words and ideas that seem so far-fetched. I hope I can be more articulate in the future.

STOP AND REFLECT

How would YOU describe the Pentecost experience to someone who had never heard of such a thing?

37. Pentecost aftermath experiences... many days later

Dear Diary,

It has been quite a while since I have been able to sit down and write. I can hardly settle my fingers to put quill to paper.

I begin here as I ended my entry about that incredible experience of being filled with the promised Holy Spirit. Jesus had told us (hmmm... maybe it was a "holy warning") that once we received that guiding Comforter, we would know exactly what to do.

Immediately after the little flames were consumed into themselves, and we managed to catch our collective breaths, we knew that we had to go out and share the promised gift with others. After hiding away in this place for our safety for so long, somehow we all knew that we would be safe when we left. It must have been almost comical to see us all trying to get out the door at the same time!!

As soon as we entered the streets that day, we met visitors from other places, and we spoke to them.[1] I can't believe I'm even writing these words, that even I (a humble "tag-along") could speak to them IN THEIR OWN LANGUAGES!! I have never studied the languages of Asia, but there were utterances coming out of my mouth and the Asian Jews understood what I was saying!! Somehow, I knew I was telling them about Jesus, because I recognized His name as I said it, even though I didn't understand the other words I was saying.

Each of us was speaking to the people in the streets in their own languages. They recognized us as Galileans by our dress... but they were surprised beyond belief that we were speaking in their languages! A couple of them thought we were drunk even though it was still early on that Sunday morning.

We are so proud of Peter! He spoke out with such authority! He stood so tall and his chest was enlarged with the confidence that stuffed him... I think I would have laughed if it weren't so serious. As the crowds gathered around him and us, Peter quoted scripture from the prophet, Joel... words that reminded the people about G*d's promise to send the Spirit upon G*d's people so they could prophesy and dream great dreams and see visions. Those hearing Peter speak recognized the words... and then Peter almost scolded them, saying if they recognized the words of prophecy, they should have realized that what they were seeing was the work of the Spirit, not mere drunkenness.

I guess that admonishment got their attention because then Peter started talking about Jesus... he talked about His life and death and resurrection, all the while quoting scripture that those faithful Jews recognized. Peter spoke with such conviction that no one realized how the time was passing. After several HOURS, Peter stopped. There wasn't a sound in the huge crowd that had gathered. One person asked what they should do with the new knowledge that Peter had made clear to them.

Peter said that they must turn their hearts and minds around and accept Jesus of Nazareth as the Messiah and as their personal Savior. Peter promised them that if they were baptized in the name of Jesus, their sins would be forgiven and they too would receive the Holy Spirit, just as we had.

Each new person is a brand-new unbelievable "event"!! Those hearers responded in droves!!! Hundreds of them moved forward at once to be baptized. Suddenly we KNEW exactly what we were to do as we baptized them... as Jesus had said: "... in the name of the Father, the Son, and the Holy Spirit." It was so simple, yet so profound! We all spent the rest of the day baptizing them and praying with them and for them. At the end of the day, as we shared our experiences, we figure that there must have been THOUSANDS of souls who responded to Peter's message.[2]

We have been in the streets and at the wells of the city for much of the time during this last week... we have been talking to people and watching them get all excited about Jesus... so excited that they run home to grab family members and neighbors to bring them back so THEY too can hear the grand Story for themselves.

Indeed, that is what we have been doing every day. Goodness! I have lost track of what day this is!

Not only Peter, but each of us has found a voice to tell the good news and stories that Jesus so often shared with us. Just when I think that I have forgotten some details of a story, something inside me reminds me of those missing points, so that everyone who listens hears the stories and scriptures accurately. And people are responding to our message... no, that's not quite what is happening... they are responding to the message that G*d's Holy Spirit is giving them through us. It is that grand Spirit that is using us as spokespeople. I can't express how exciting this is. At the end of the day, we are exhausted, but at the same time, so energized that it's hard to sleep. We can't wait for the sun to rise on a new day to go out and meet more people and share this extraordinary experience!

Again I feel that my words are terribly insufficient to express the excitement of all this. I pray that each person we meet will somehow hear our experience with Jesus... and will allow the precious Holy Spirit to take control of their lives.

This is all so very different from what I expected. In truth, I didn't know WHAT I expected... it certainly wasn't this. I know my troubles are not over, but I feel certain that I can face ANYTHING, because I am safe in G*od's mighty hands.

38. Scattering

Dear Diary,

A while ago, we imagined that we couldn't possibly stay in Jerusalem to make a living... now we realize that indeed we cannot possibly stay here to have a life as Jesus modeled for us. Our need to remain cooped up in this place that has been our safety for these many weeks is overpowered by the tugs on our hearts to leave and face the unknown in other places. As Jesus said: to "Judea... Samaria... and the remotest places on this earth."

As we reflected on it, it seems more and more appropriate that the Holy Spirit came to us during the Festival of Weeks. Ancient prophecy described those who were to be invited to "the feast" during that festival some 50 days after Passover;[1] they included servants, sons AND daughters, Levites, the fatherless, the widow, the stranger. The Israelites were to be reminded of what it was like to be slaves in Egypt. Just how far would this extravagant invitation extend... to the shunned? the foreigner? the lonely? the shamed? the deformed?... oh my goodness... could Gentiles and even pagans be included??

HOW CAN THIS BE??? How are we to know if what we think we are hearing and thinking is what G*d is intending for us? How will we know if and when we are ready for... for... whatever we are supposed to be ready for?

It seemed that every time we dug into our ancient writings for guidance, one overwhelming message came to us. We were reminded that our G*d spoke to our ancient father Abraham saying: "Do not fear, for I am always with you. I will bless you..."[2]

Cleopas reminded us of his experience with Jesus on that resurrection day. He and his brother didn't recognize Jesus who was walking right there with them. Even when they said to Jesus' face that they were disappointed in all that had led to His ending, Jesus stayed with them and spoke to them, opening their minds and calming their grieving hearts to the reality of the situation. "I felt my heart BURNING as He walked with us.[3] I feel my heart BURNING in the same way right now. I'm not a speaker like Peter, but I feel some kind of a tug in my soul that I should be going somewhere and speaking to others. I can't explain it... but I feel the same joy and excitement... and quite frankly the same apprehension that I felt that day when I ran all the way back here to tell you my news. I can't express complicated religious concepts, but I CAN share what I have experienced personally. I'm not sure where I'm supposed to be going or what I should be doing, but I feel that I can rely on Jesus somehow being with me no matter what road I am traveling. There are people back in Emmaus who still don't believe... I will start there."

With a bit of hesitation, Thomas talked about Jesus knowing exactly what he needed... knowing that he had to TOUCH the scars on Jesus' hands and side in order to conquer his own doubting heart. Now Thomas is certain that Jesus will somehow continue to fill all his needs as he moves out. "I have never even thought of traveling to the Far East... now I have no doubt that I am supposed to head in that direction."[4]

Peter has been such a powerful witness to Jesus here in Jerusalem in these last days. "Jesus saw through my stubbornness and hard-headedness. After my abysmal actions during His trial, I really didn't deserve the blessing of being among the very first to witness His resurrection. My Lord Jesus allowed me to reverse my denial... when He commanded me: 'feed My sheep' and 'care for My lambs.' At that time, I didn't know how to be a shepherd, but after these experiences here in Jerusalem, I am sure that I should be stretching the borders of my teaching and preaching. I am bursting with love for Jesus, sent by our G*d... and I'm learning to listen and trust this new Spirit that is coming to fill us and guide us. My soul needs to proclaim my own transformation as I reach out to those who are considered 'unclean' and 'unworthy' in the eyes of the so-called 'religious authorities'. I will begin by moving out to Samaria, so I can still be close to those of you who remain here in Jerusalem."[5]

John spoke up: "Do you remember when Jesus told us: 'Let not your hearts be troubled and do not be afraid. My peace I give you... not the peace as the world gives... but MY PEACE I GIVE TO YOU.'[6]? I believe Jesus meant that HIS peace would be different... maybe not even easy or quiet or calm. And I believe that He meant for us to depend on G*d's true peace even in the midst of turmoil and trouble. Once, Jesus called me and my brother James 'the Sons of Thunder'[7]... no doubt recognizing our fiery and stormy temperaments. I cherish the fact that Jesus entrusted His mother into my care; I hope that meant He had trust in my modified character. I will care for Mary for as long as I live. I believe that I am being led to move up into Asia Minor to continue our mission in G*D'S peace."[8]

Matthias admitted that he was terrified when our group... or more rightly, our G*d... chose him to be the disciples' replacement in this ministry. He went on to confess that now he is trembling in a very different way. "I was privileged to be among the seventy that Jesus sent out on an exploratory mission so long ago. We went in pairs back then... and experienced the highs and lows of teaching and healing. I pray that I have learned enough during these last days here in Jerusalem to go out... alone. But I KNOW I WILL NOT BE ALONE! During our teachings here in the city during the Festival of Weeks, I met a number of people who had journeyed up from Ethiopia; they were receptive to our message and even said they wished that more of their family members had come to be able to hear all this. I feel I can be of value if I head to Ethiopia. I hope that I will still be able to speak in their language as I travel there; I will trust the Holy Spirit to continue to put the right words into my mouth."[9]

This same message is coming over and over:[10]

"Do not be afraid, for I will go with you and I will rescue you."

"My LORD is my shepherd... I shall not fear."

I have to chuckle a little, for once... to "test" our search for direction in the ancient writings, we pulled one portion at random... unrolled it at random... and pointed to a random verse. Our hearts raced with awe when the leader read: "G*d said, 'You are my servants; I have chosen you. So do not fear, for I am with you; do not be dismayed, for I am your G*d. I will strengthen you and help you; I will uphold you with my righteous right hand.'[11]" WHY am I not surprised that our G*d would see right through our little scheme to "test" the scriptural answers?

As the days go by, one by one.... buoyed by this repeated message... another member of our "family" declares an intention to move on. It seems that each one is receiving a different, personal message; the consistency is in the certainty that G*d's Spirit is at work. Each time, we gather around, laying our hands on that precious friend as they answer that "tug at the heart". Our leaders were the first to resolutely make their way into their respective futures. As they have done so, we miss their constant leadership, but their firm witness remains with us. We continue to pray and listen for discernment for the rest of us.

It is James who has steadied us. He firmly feels that his future is to remain here in Jerusalem. "It didn't seem to matter to Jesus that, for so long, I had been foolish in not recognizing the true identity of my older brother. He assured me that He believed that I would go on to do great things. It didn't make much sense before He left my presence at that time... but my future is beginning to be clearer now. The ground in this city feels different... could it be (like Moses experienced) that this is not just a religious center, but truly Holy Ground?"[12]

As each person is able to articulate that "tug in their souls" and has gathered their meager possessions in preparation to leave us, we sense an excitement with very little trepidation. This is all happening pretty quickly... and there seems to be a "rightness" in it all.

I really hope that we can somehow continue to communicate with each other to know what is happening and how this whole continued ministry of our Lord Jesus Christ is progressing. I guess I'm assuming that it WILL progress. We'll see.

I haven't yet felt that "certainty of heart" that some of the others have expressed. I admit that I'm not able to completely squelch my inner fear... but my sense of trust is growing as I hear others' descriptions of clear discernment of their purpose and plan. Our G*d is so good!

STOP AND REFLECT

DO NOT FEAR!
The promised Holy Spirit is acting in ways that no one expected. The followers are responding to the various tugs on their hearts. Until recently, they complained about the crowded conditions and now... they are splitting up as they wade into the unknown. They are armed only with the conviction that they need not fear. What does that say to your heart?

---

39. Into my own future

Dear Diary,

Before he left, John reassured us that just because some have heard G*d speaking to them earlier than others by NO MEANS indicates that our personal pathway is inferior. I really appreciate that. John carefully reminded us that, while on the cross, even our most-faithful Jesus desperately prayed when His Abba G*d's voice seemed absent.[1]

In the past, I have made no secret of my admiration for Mary Magdalene. I continue to be amazed by this woman... this WOMAN... who has been such a valued and trusted disciple of Jesus. Although she was not among the twelve "chosen", I really wish she had been nominated as a replacement for "the betrayer" (hmmm... how long will it before we might understand his motivations and purpose so we can truly forgive him and say his name?)

Mary has LONG spoken of the great privilege that Jesus considered her to be an equal member of this "family". Jesus turned so many old traditions "topsy-turvy": the first would be last... a master is no more than the servant... a humbly-given mite is a huge offering... the least are as blessed as the powerful... a woman is a precious being in her own right.

Mary is now feeling the nudge to return to Magdala and find a dwelling place big enough to offer a safe haven to women who are abused and neglected by husbands and families and who are disparaged by society... and have no other hope. THAT is such a radical notion and will make such an impact! No doubt, there will be MUCH push-back from most men, who, of course, will be defended by the authorities. Just this idea makes me smile in anticipation![2]

At first, I asked Mary if I might accompany her on this mission. We prayed about it... and, after much frustration, agreed that that was not my personal "tug". More and more, dear Hannah and I seemed to be moving in the same direction. For many sad reasons, Hannah has no home or family to return to.

My home city of Capernaum[3] has kept coming into our thoughts. It was there where I first met Jesus. He had called fishermen from Capernaum as His first disciples. For quite a while, He centered His ministry there, even calling it "My own city". For all Jesus' healing and teaching there, most residents didn't respond to His message. My family expressed only mild curiosity when I first spoke of my interest in Jesus' teaching... and their response was vehemently against Jesus when I declared that I wanted to join His group as they traveled. At one point, Jesus criticized my hometown for its refusal to accept His message... and went so far as to curse Capernaum for its lack of faith.[4]

As I remembered Peter's cool reception when he and the other fishermen returned to Capernaum after our Lord's resurrection, I find myself really resisting the idea of returning to face my own family. As much as I want to respond to G*d's tug on my heart, I also feel the urge to run (fast) in ANY direction other than toward Capernaum. I don't remember hearing the others express this dilemma; I so want and need to talk to someone else! But... it seemed that all other alternatives were closed off. Much to my chagrin, I think I am supposed to accept the idea that I am to return to my family. Would Capernaum really become my "home" again?

Oh REALLY?? A future for me in Capernaum? Deep down my guts scream: "Here I am, Lord Almighty... please send Hannah!"

Thankfully Hannah has stayed with me, and we have traveled slowly as we head into the Galilee region. WHY were my feet so heavy when the "tug on my heart" seemed to come as clearly as it did? WHY was I so slow to accept this leap of faith into my own future? How I wished my response were different!

When we arrived at my old home, I hesitated. Hannah and I prayed again. Would my family welcome me... or pretend that they didn't even know me anymore? Would they listen to our stories or insist that they were right about my "senseless" decision to follow Jesus?

I was trembling with such uncertainty that I actually KNOCKED on the door of my own "home". My mother answered and hardly hesitated before enveloping me in her arms. My father (and my brothers still living at home) were "frosty". They all sat silently with their arms crossed as my mother hustled around to offer us food. I was ready to turn around and leave immediately when... out of the corner of my eye... I saw a dove alight at the open window behind my father. I know Hannah saw it too, because there were tears in her eyes. (I remembered Jesus' account of doves appearing to bring His Father's message at certain times of His own life.[5]) My ears didn't hear any voice, but the message to my heart was absolutely clear.

This was the "right" choice; this is the beginning of my future.

40. My place in Capernaum

Dear Diary,

     Hannah and I have been here with my family for some time now. I still think twice before calling this house my "home"... it's the same place, but such a different relationship!

     After a short period of coolness, my family really started listening to us as we shared story after story. I was pleasantly surprised that they continued to be interested in all that has happened. I felt like Peter (and Mary Magdalene) were sitting on my shoulders whispering in my ears in that Hannah and I were able to answer many of the questions that were asked. Of course, my family (and the neighbors) had heard all about Jesus' death and the reports of His resurrection. They had expected to see me soon after that, figuring I would have finally come to my senses and would have needed to escape the danger posed in Jerusalem. They had even heard reports from people traveling through Capernaum back to their homes after their experiences during the Festival of Weeks in the Holy City.

     After a number of days (oh, we have lost track of how long we have been here!), my father expressed his thought that Hannah and I should take advantage of the fact that Capernaum is on a major trade route of people traveling between the East and Jerusalem. I must admit my dismay, because at first I thought he was still expressing some of his misgivings about my return... and was suggesting that we needed to find some form of employment with any one of the many hostels meeting the local needs of those travelers. But NO! He realized that we were talking about a much larger concept than feeding travelers' stomachs and providing rest for travelers' bodies. As he was expressing these thoughts, my heart started to beat much faster and began to SING! My father... MY OWN FATHER HAD HEARD THE MESSAGE that we had hardly dared to express!!!

I was ASTOUNDED as my father (of all people!) remembered the stories we told about our dear friends, Mary and Martha, who had extended gracious hospitality to Jesus and all of us. Then it was MY FATHER (my goodness!) who suggested that Hannah and I should explore some similar form of hospitality here in Capernaum, where we could share our stories... and Spirit... as well as much-needed lodging.

I NEVER expected to see my own father's mouth open... and hear our G*d's voice coming out!!

So... it seems that I am no longer merely a "Jesus tag-along." I am growing. I am a follower of my Lord Jesus Christ. I am a messenger. I even dare to claim that I am an apostle, sent to spread the great "good news" of G*d's kingdom. In spite of Jesus' curse on Capernaum, I entertain the possibility that even here, I am walking on Holy Ground.

I am empowered. I close the pages of this diary... and will open a very different accounting of events and people and relationships that will (hopefully) reflect my own ministry.[1]

YES! Our G*d is good! All the time!

Shalom chaverim. L'hitra'ot. May we all live in peace!

STOP AND REFLECT

Thank you for accompanying me and the "tag-along" on this journey. I hope that you have taken some time along the way to reflect on your own participation during those awesome and tumultuous days of long ago that, in some ways, seem so contemporary.

ENDNOTES

Scriptural citations for events and other clarifying NOTES are
indicated in the diary entries with a number linking
to the endnote in that entry.

Entry 1. My beginning

[1] Jesus calls the first four disciples: Mark 1:14-19; Matthew 4:18-21. John's account (1:35-48) also goes on to name others.

[2] *NOTE: names of all twelve of "the chosen" are listed in Matthew 10:1-4 as they are being sent out; there's no specific scriptural information about Jesus calling them.*

Entry 2. Into Jericho

[1] Read the whole episode about blind Bartimaeus: Mark 10:46-52.

[2] Read the entire story of Zaccheus: John 11.

Entry 3. Sabbath

[1] *NOTE about the Sabbath: As God commanded, the Sabbath (on the seventh day of the week) is a day of rest. The Sabbath begins at sundown on Friday and ends at sundown on Saturday. All work is forbidden, except deeds of mercy, acts of necessity, and worship. Read the Sabbath promise in Isaiah 58:13-14. The Sabbath observance is a family affair; traditionally the mother of the family calls everyone to light the Sabbath candles to begin.*

[2] Check out the story in Matthew 12:1-13 when Jesus breaks Sabbath "rules".

Entry 4. At Bethany

[1] The home of Lazarus and his sisters, Mary and Martha. Evidently Jesus and friends often visited in this home. The sisters served different roles as they cared for guests.

[2] Read the entire account Lazarus' death and burial, and then being raised from the grave: John 11:1-44.

[3] Check out Luke 10:38-42 for an account of a clash between the two sisters.

[4] Mary anointing Jesus with nard: John 12:1-7

[5] *NOTE about this "anointing" with perfumed nard: Mark 14:1-6 recounts the same act, but at another place and time, by a different woman. There are a number of instances where the same act is recalled in different ways. It's unsure whether these are multiple acts, or different memories of the gospel writers.*

Entry 5. Entry into Jerusalem

1 Jesus needing a colt: Luke 19:28-34 and Mark 11:1-12. Matthew's account (21:1-6) includes the reference to Isaiah 62:11, predicting that the King would come riding a donkey (not a white horse). John's account (12:12-19) cites Zechariah's prophecy about the colt.

2 Cloaks thrown on the road and shouts of "Hosanna": Luke 19:35-38, Mark 11:7-10, Matthew 21:7-11 and John 12:12-13.

3 Among the Old Testament prophecies is Zechariah 9:9, claiming that "your king will come riding on a colt."

4 Pharisees ordering Jesus to stop the noise: Luke 19:39-40. See also the reaction of Pharisees in John 21:17-19.

5 Jesus cries at sight of Holy City: Luke 19:41-44.

6 *NOTE although this "Triumphal entry" is recorded in all four gospels, the details differ some, perhaps indicating differences in the memories of the writers or showing what they thought was more important.*

Entry 6. Fig tree and cleansing the Temple

1 Entire episode of the withering of fig tree and efficacy of prayer: Matthew 21: 18-22 and Mark 11:20-25

2 *NOTE about the Temple: the majority of area of the Great Temple was the enormous "Court of the Gentiles" where ANYONE of any age could enter; the stalls of the merchants and the money-changers were tucked into covered area in the outer walls of this area. The next smaller area was the "Court of the Women" where anyone BORN JEWISH could enter. The next even smaller area was the open "Court of the Israelites, where only JEWISH MEN could enter to offer their sacrifices at the large altar there. The "Sanctuary" was a closed structure built at the far end of the whole Temple area and was open only to PRIESTS "on duty". At the front of that inner temple was "the Holy of Holies" where God resided and where only the High Priest dared to enter once a year to beg for forgiveness on the behalf of all Jews.*

3 *NOTE about the "businesses" set up in the outer Temple area. Visitors traveling long distances could not bring with them the necessary unblemished animals needed for sacrifice; they depended on the merchants at the Temple for purchase of the sacrificial animals. Likewise, "foreign" money could be exchanged.*

4 *NOTE about the clearing of the Temple: the gospels differ about the timing of clearing of the Temple by Jesus. Mark (11:12-19) indicates that everyone went back to Bethany on Sunday, only to return to Jerusalem the next day, while the other gospels indicate that Jesus cleared the Temple area immediately after entering the city hailed with palm branches and shouts of "Hosanna".*

5 NOTE about "the blind and the lame": any Jew would readily understand this prohibition of the blind and lame. Since the time of Moses, no deformed man was allowed to serve as a priest in the Temple (Lev. 21:16-31). According to history, David's army was held in contempt by the Jesubites (who claimed the high land that David sought) saying that "even the blind and the crippled could keep them out of the city." When David established centralized worship in the Temple in Jerusalem, he certainly remembered those mocking words. David returned that sense of contempt and declared that no physically disabled person had any business whatsoever to ever go beyond the outer Court of the Gentiles to enter into the sacred inner courts (2 Samuel 5:6-8). In healing these blind and lame, Jesus' act would fly in the face of thousands of years of Hebrew religious tradition.

Entry 7. Facing the Pharisees

1 NOTE about this whole debate between Jesus and the Temple leaders: although Jesus aimed His responses at the Pharisees, the disciples were also learning and (hopefully) understanding more.

2 Reaction of the Pharisees who questioned Jesus' authority is reported (Luke 20:1-8; Matthew 21:23-27; and Mark 11:27-33) Not the same questions/responses are recorded in the different gospels.

3 The Parable of the Vineyard Owner is recorded in Luke 20:9-19. (The owner's son was sent to check on the harvest and was killed by the tenants.)

Entry 8. More teachings

1 The lessons continue: Luke 20:9- 21:38; Matthew 21:28-25:46 and Mark 12:1–13:37. As you read these, remember the urgency with which they are being taught.

2 NOTE about the lessons listed above: each gospel recounts what some of these lessons meant for the disciples. In these (what will be) last days, Jesus' teachings are more earnest and somber. Mark and Luke had previously recorded many of Jesus' parables and story-lessons.

3 NOTE about the Passover: Passover is one of the three great Hebrew festivals. It commemorates the sacrifice of a lamb to protect the Hebrew people when they were slaves in Egypt. Hebrews smeared blood on their doorposts to show God which homes to "pass over" when God destroyed every first-born in the effort to persuade the Pharaoh the let God's Hebrew sons and daughters go. It was a meal prepared in haste as the Hebrews had no time to make proper bread before the Pharoah's decree of freedom, commanding them to leave Egypt immediately.

⁴ NOTE *about the Passover celebration: in Jesus' time, Passover had become a pilgrim celebration. The traditional Jewish ritual that is still used today at a Passover Seder was already in place. Large numbers of people flocked to Jerusalem to observe the annual commemoration. Jesus and his entourage ate the Passover meal together on the eve of his death. Like the blood of the lamb that had saved the people from destruction in Egypt, it was the blood of Jesus, that perfect sacrifice, that redeems all people from the power and bond of sin and death.*

Entry 9. Passover meal, Garden of Gethsemane, Jesus' arrest

¹ Preparations for the gathering: a man carrying water (Luke 22:10) was highly unusual because carrying water was a woman's task.

² Washing the guests' feet was the customary act of welcome into a home; it was normally the task of a servant or a young daughter. In John's gospel (13:1-17), Jesus makes the point that no master is greater than the servant... and that all disciples needed to love and serve each other.

³ Prediction of the betrayal: Matthew 26:14-16; 20-25; Mark 14:17-21; and Luke 22:1-6 all tell of Judas' plan to betray Jesus to the religious leaders. At the table Jesus called Judas out as the one who would betray Him and told him to leave and carry out that task. As despicable as was this betrayal, it was necessary to carry out all the prophecies from ancient times.

⁴ The Last Supper: In Luke 22:14-20; Mark 14:22-23 and Matthew 26:26-29, Jesus strayed from the Passover ritual as He gave extraordinary meaning to the broken bread and the shared wine. These few verses are the basis for our Communion Feast.

⁵ Prediction of Peter's denial is foretold in all four gospels: Matthew 26:31-35; Mark 14:27-31; Luke 22:31-34; and John 13:31-38.

⁶ Garden of Gethsemane is on the side of a hill across a great valley from the city. It was an olive garden and press to make precious olive oil. It was generally cool in the shade of the twisted olive trees. Jesus asked His disciples to watch from afar as He prayed (Matthew 26:36-46; Luke 22:39-46; Mark 14:32-42). John (17:1-25) recounts the prayers that Jesus offered (however these could have been imagined).

⁷ Jesus' arrest is reported in all four gospels (Matthew 26:47-56; Mark 14:43-52; Luke 22:47-52; and John 18:1-11)... interestingly each with slightly different details.

Entry 10. Trial at Sanhedrin; before Pilate, before Herod; the crucifixion; hasty burial

1 NOTE about the religious court: the Sanhedrin was the highest court of religious justice, made up of the more than seventy prominent religious leaders. Although they adjudicated cases of religious issues, they had limited power to sentence a prisoner to death. After their preliminary charges of blasphemy, it was necessary to send Jesus to the Roman leader, Pontius Pilate and the Jewish figurehead governor, Herod.

2 Testimony before the Sanhedrin was contradictory and inconclusive, but the court was determined to find Jesus guilty as reported in Matthew 26: 57-57; Mark 14: 53-65; and John 18: 12-14 and 19-24. Luke 22: 54 simply states that Jesus appeared before the religious leaders.

3 NOTE about the "pit": it was common knowledge that accused people brought before the Sanhedrin were confined, not in a cell, but in a small, dark pit dug below the meeting place of the Council, while the religious leaders deliberated their fate. The accused was thrown into that pit that was accessible only by means of a ladder.

4 Jesus appears before Pilate: this Roman leader knew he was in a tough spot and did not want to kill Jesus. He tried to use Passover custom of releasing one prisoner, but the people gathered shouted for Barabbas to be released. Matthew 27:11-26 and Mark 15:1-15

5 In an effort to "pass the buck", Pilate sent Jesus out to Herod, the puppet Jewish "king" who only wanted Jesus to perform some miracle in his presence… and who then sent Jesus back to Pilate. Pilate washed his hands in front of the crowd, symbolizing that he was not responsible for Jesus' death. Nevertheless, Pilate was required to order Jesus' crucifixion. John 18: 28-40 and 19:1-16; and Luke 22:56-73 record the back and forth between Pilate and Herod.

6 Soldiers' treatment of Jesus: after being condemned to be crucified, Jesus was mocked by the attending soldiers and ordered to carry his own cross through the streets of Jerusalem from Pilate's palace out to place called Golgotha (less than one-half mile). The gospels record the crucifixion, as Jesus was on the cross, hanging between two thieves. Also recorded are the several aspects that were foretold by ancient prophets, like no broken bones (usually done to hasten the death), the darkness and earthquake, the tearing of the Temple veil (that had traditionally separated God from God's people), and the gambling of Jesus' cloak. Matthew 27:27-56; Mark 15:16-41; Luke 23:1-49; John 18:26-19:30.

7 Stranger ordered to help carry Jesus' cross: Matthew notes (15:32) that a man from Cyrene (probably in Jerusalem for the Passover commemoration) was picked out of the crowd to help Jesus carry the heavy cross.

8 *NOTE: The traditional Stations of the Cross mark several stops along Jesus' walk across Jerusalem after being condemned. The Cyrene helping to carry the cross is one station that is cited in Matthew's account. Several other stations (Jesus meeting His mother along the way, Veronica wiping His face, and the kindness of another woman) are not recorded in scripture; rather, they mark tradition and scriptural imagination, much like this journey of a "tag-along".*

9 *NOTE: Traditionally, there are seven statements made by Jesus from the cross:*

> *"I am thirsty." (Matthew 19:28)*
>
> *"Father, forgive them, for they don't know what they are doing." (Luke 23:34)*
>
> *"My God, why have you forsaken me?" (Matthew 15:46 and Mark 15:45)*
>
> *"Dear woman, here is your son." (to his mother) and "Here is your mother." (to a beloved disciple, generally agreed to be John. John 19:25-27)*
>
> *"I tell you the truth, today you will be with me in paradise." (to the thief hanging on cross next to Him, Luke 23:43)*
>
> *"Father, into your hands I commend my spirit." (Luke 23:46)*
>
> *"It is finished" (John 19:30)*

10 Jesus' death was fast. Crucifixion is such a cruel manner of torture and execution. Criminals are either nailed or tied to the cross and left to die. Sometimes it took days (even after being beaten) for the condemned to die from exhaustion and asphyxiation. Blood cannot circulate and the body is crushed by its own weight. Leg bones are usually broken, so the condemned can't find any relief at all, but Jesus was already dead by the time the soldiers started to break leg bones of the others (John 19:31-37). This fulfills the prophecy (Psalm 34:20) that the legs of the one sent by God would not be broken, although the side would be pierced. By tradition, Jesus hung on the cross for three hours.

11 The earthquake: scripture recounts (Matthew 27:50-53) that at the moment that Jesus died, an earthquake shook the world and the sky went dark (even in the middle of the day).

12 Joseph of Arimathea was a religious leader, a member of the Sanhedrin. Evidently it was known that he was in favor of

Jesus, so he was not summoned to the hastily-called court session after Jesus was arrested. Normally, the dead are left on the cross to be eaten by scavengers, but Joseph took a great risk to ask for Jesus' body. He and Nicodemus buried Jesus in Joseph's new tomb that was near the place of the crucifixion. Preparations were limited by the fact that it was late on Friday and the burial had to be done before the Sabbath began. (Matthew 27:57-61; Mark 15:42-47; Luke 23:50-56; John 20:38-42)

13 *NOTE: we now call this day "Good Friday", not that there seemed to be any good in it at that time. A better name might be: "God's Friday"*

Entry 11. After the end of the Sabbath

1 Peter's denial of Jesus: Matthew 26:69-75; Mark 14:66-72; Luke 23:54-62; John 18:15-18 and 25-27 all record the events in the courtyard during Jesus' trial before the Sanhedrin.

2 When Jesus called him as a disciple, his given name was Simon. When Peter was the first disciple to recognize Jesus as the Messiah (Matthew 16:13-17), Jesus renamed him "Peter" (meaning "the rock"). Peter's character was not always rock-like (as in this episode of denial), but it did indicate the person that Peter would become, by God's grace.

3 Matthew (27:62-66) tells of the orders from Pilate to post guards at the sealed tomb, lest Jesus' body be stolen.

4 See NOTE in Entry 10, recording what Jesus is heard saying while hanging on the cross.

Entry 12. Early on the first day of the week

1 The wise men saw the star announcing the birth of a new king and traveled to Bethlehem to find the Baby Jesus and His parents. Traditionally they brought gifts of gold, frankincense and myrrh (Matthew 2:1-12)

2 Prediction of great grief to Mary: when Mary and Joseph presented Jesus at the Temple when He was eight days old (Luke 2:21-40), an old man (Simeon) recognized Jesus' true identity. As he blessed the parents, he predicted that Mary's heart would ultimately be pierced by a sword (v. 35).

3 *NOTE: Three Marys: the gospels differ as to the identity of the women who went to the tombsite early on that morning.*

4 Intent on giving Jesus a more proper burial, the main concern of those women was how to enter the tomb. (Matthew 28:1; Mark 16:1-3; Luke 24:1) John identifies only Mary Magdalene as the woman approaching the tomb area.

Entry 13. Late on the day of resurrection

1 The records of the Resurrection give different details about the events and what happened. Luke (24:1-12) and Matthew (28:1-8) are similar, with the women going back to tell the other disciples and Peter running to the empty tomb. Jesus' messages are a little different in each gospel.

2 *NOTE: John (20:7) devotes this verse to the tiny detail that the napkin which had been placed over Jesus' face was carefully folded and placed aside from the other grave clothes. Any Jew would recognize the significance. When a table was set exactly, the servant would stand aside until the master finished eating. If the master was done eating, he would rise from the table, wipe his fingers and mouth, wad up that napkin and toss it onto the table. The wadded napkin meant: "I'm done" and servant would then clear the table. But if the master rose from the table, folded his napkin, laying it beside his plate, the servant would not dare touch the table, because the folded napkin meant: "I'm not finished yet." It meant, "I'm coming back!"*

3 John recounts (John 20:1-18) that Mary Magdalene was alone to see the empty tomb. She went back to the disciples to alert the others and Peter ran back to the tomb to see for himself. Only after he left to report to all the others did Mary Magdalene speak with Jesus (whom she first thought was the gardener); she recognized Jesus only after He called her by name.

4 *NOTE: Mark's account ends abruptly with the angels announcing that Jesus was no longer in the tomb, but telling the women to advise the others that Jesus would "go ahead and meet them in Galilee". Most reliable manuscripts from Mark END by saying that the women didn't say anything, because they were so afraid. Note that other writers, considering Mark's account incomplete probably added "a better ending" to Mark's original account.*

Entry 14. Judas

1 Judas conspires with the religious leaders to betray Jesus: Matthew 26:14-16; Mark 14:10-11; Luke 22:1-5. John (13:18-30) recalls Jesus' prediction of the betrayal at the Last Supper.

2 Judas hanged himself after trying to return the money he had received from the religious leaders (Matthew 27:1-10)

3 *NOTE Deuteronomy 21:22-23 declares that anyone who is hung on a tree is cursed by God, so Judas chose this extra curse upon himself, adding to the prohibition of suicide. Jesus' apostles applied the phrase "hanging on a tree" and that connected curse to Jesus' death (Acts 5:30 and Galatians 3:13), adding that Jesus transformed that dishonorable way*

of death into a beautiful image of God's sacrificial and redeeming love.
4 Jesus' words from the cross; again refer back to notes in Entry 10.

Entry 15. Cleopas and his brother

1 Luke (24:13-36) is the only gospel writer who relates this story about the encounter on the road to Emmaus (some seven miles from Jerusalem). Scripture only identifies Cleopas' companion as "another man"; tradition says he was Cleopas' brother. This tag-along has given the brother the name "Felix".

2 *NOTE: again, Mark's gospel ends abruptly at the tomb site and only an "unreliable" addition describes the appearance of Jesus to any of the followers.*

Entry 16. Mary Magdalene

1 This story about Mary Magdalene is not recounted in scripture, but rather a reflection of this diarist.

Entry 17. Jesus' appearance

1 Jesus' appearance to the gathered followers is recounted in Luke 24:36-49 and John 20:19-23. Note again that Mark's most reliable manuscripts do not include any accounts of Jesus appearing to His followers.

Entry 18. Community

1 This is purely a reflection of this diarist of what it might have been like with all those followers trying to stay together.

Entry 19. The next Sunday

1 Matthew (24:11-15) recounts that the religious authorities feared that the disciples would steal Jesus' body and announce that He had risen from the dead. They appealed to Pilate, who ordered the tomb to be sealed and guards posted. Evidently the guards couldn't account for what had happened; each told a different story.

2 Luke 23:44,45 and Mark 15:38 mention (almost in passing) that at the moment of Jesus' death, "darkness came over the land, and the veil in the Temple was torn in two".

3 *NOTE: That veil (a heavy curtain) separated the Holy of Holies in the most sacred inner room of the Temple, where it was believed that was the enthronement room of God. Tradition required that ONLY the High Priest could enter that place ONLY on the one day of the year of Yom Kippur to beg for the forgiveness of all the Hebrew people; any other*

entrance was punishable by death. Although this damage deep inside the Temple was not visible to most worshipers, there must have been great consternation among the religious authorities. The tearing of that separating veil indicated that Jesus had opened the way for all people to freely approach God.

Entry 20. Retelling stories

1 Again this is a reflection of this diarist of the possible activities of the gathered community.

2 *NOTE: Mark is believed to the first to write down the events of Jesus' life. His account stresses facts and actions (rather than themes or topics), focusing on Jesus's many miracles. Although the shortest, it is often the most detailed. Almost half of Mark's writing deals with the events of the last week of Jesus' earthly life (again, ending abruptly in the death and shortened resurrection account).*

Entry 21. Visit from the Roman soldier

1 One centurion among those in the crucifixion detail proclaimed Jesus' identity (Matthew 27:54). The rest of this entry is another reflection of this diarist.

Entry 22. Centurion returns with companion

1 All four gospels (Matthew 27:35; Mark 15:24b; Luke 23:34b) record that the soldiers cast lots for the robe. Further, John (19:23-24) gives the full Old Testament scriptural background that the Psalmist (22:18) had prophesied that the Messiah's garments would be divided by casting lots. This is yet another instance in which the ancient prophecies were fulfilled, even at the crucifixion.

2 *NOTE: similar to drawing straws or throwing dice, casting lots was a popular way to make decisions in biblical times. It was more common in the Old Testament, when it seemed that this "game of chance" had God's approval.*

Entry 23. Jesus appears to disciples with Thomas

1 John is the only gospel to report this episode with Thomas present (John 21:24-29)

Entry 24. Visit from Joseph of Arimathea

1 In their gospels, both Matthew (27:57) and John (19:38) refer to Joseph as a follower or disciple, and Mark (15:43) and Luke (23:50) identify him as a member of the Council. John also

relates (19:39) that Nicodemus was present at the trial before the Sanhedrin.

2 The burial is recorded is all four gospels: Matthew 27:57-61; Mark 15:42-47; Luke 23:50-54; and John 19:28-42 with some differences in details.

3 Nicodemus had taken the time to buy spices (John 19:39).

Entry 25. Questions

1 There is no scriptural basis for this episode. This diarist can only assume that such a diverse group of people probably had difficulties as they stayed in hiding.

2 Jesus' cousin, John (who came to be known as John the Baptist because of his message, related in Matthew 3:1-12; Mark 1:1-8; and Luke 3:1-18) is said to have "prepared the way" for baptism as a sign of repentance of sin. John also baptized Jesus (Matthew 3:13-17; Mark 1:9-11; and Luke 3:21-22 each with slightly different details).

3 The excuses of our biblical heroes are real: Moses who is thought to have a speech impediment, was assured that his brother Aaron would accompany him to speak. (Exodus 3:11). Read about the others mentioned: Isaiah (Isaiah 6:4; Jeremiah (Jeremiah 1: 6) and Jonah (Jonah 1:1-3).Even from the cross, Jesus seemed to be doubting His mission (Matthew 27:46).

Entry 26 Barabbas

1 Mark 15:6-15 and Luke 23:18-25 both tell of the people choosing between Jesus and Barabbas before Pilate; Matthew 27:15-26 adds the explanation that it was the Roman governor's custom to release a prisoner during the Passover feast, as a good-will gesture.

2 Mark 9:38-41 recounts the episode when the disciples questioned the validity of someone casting out demons in Jesus' name.

3 Again, there is no scriptural basis for this story about Barabbas giving witness to Jesus. Such a dramatic turn-around would be a worthy story!!

Entry 27. Lazarus and Mary

1 Again, there is no scriptural basis for this "visit".

2 Lazarus' death and burial, and then being raised from the grave is recounted in John 11:1-44

Entry 28. Nicodemus

1 The entire episode of the night-time meeting of Jesus and Nicodemus is recounted in John 3:1-21.

2 John 3:16 ("For God so loved the world...") is perhaps one of the most memorized and quoted verses of scripture.

3 Nicodemus tried to stand up for Jesus before the Sanhedrin (John 7:51), using the same rules the religious leaders were using against Jesus.

4 Again, the accounts of Jesus' burial by Nicodemus and Joseph is recorded is all four gospels: Matthew 27:57-61; Mark 15:42-47; Luke 23:50-54; and John 19:28-42 with some differences in details.

5 There is no scriptural basis for this visit from Nicodemus to the gathered followers.

Entry 29. Fishermen return from the Galilee

1 John is the only gospel writer to give this account (21:1-13), although right after His resurrection, Jesus had told Mary Magdalene to tell "the others" that He would go before them into Galilee and meet them there. (Matthew 28:7)

Entry 30. "Do you love me, Peter?"

1 Matthew 14 (22-32) recounts the story of Jesus calling Peter to walk on the water towards Him.

2 John 21:15-17 continues the episode of the disciples meeting Jesus on the beach. Jesus specifically addressed Peter asking to affirm his love (three times) and commanding him to care for Jesus' sheep.

3 In John 21:18-23, Peter challenged Jesus about the future of Judas, who had betrayed Jesus. Jesus rebuked Peter, saying essentially that it was no concern of any one whom Jesus chooses to redeem.

4 Previously, in the midst of teaching (Matthew 16:13-16), Jesus had asked His disciples about the identity of the "Son of Man". Peter spoke right up to affirm Jesus, and He responded by renaming Simon as "Peter", the rock on which Jesus would build His church (Matthew 16:13-19).

5 Immediately following being named "Peter" (Matthew 16:21-23), Peter began to rebuke Jesus for speaking about His death. Jesus then turned to Peter and changed his name again, saying "Satan, get behind me. You are a stumbling block to me."

6 NOTE: *When there is a change of names in scripture, pay close attention, because it usually meant a big change in the life of the one named. Among*

others, think of Abram to Abraham (Genesis 17:5), Jacob to Israel (Genesis 32:22-32), Saul to Paul (Acts 9). Simon Peter's struggle with his name paralleled his struggle with his identity until he acknowledged, after Jesus redeemed him, that he was REALLY Peter (the rock).

Entry 31. James

1 NOTE: Sons of Joseph and Mary: James, Joseph, Simon, and Judas. They are named in different events (there are also some sisters who are not named). In the early church, there was an attempt to proclaim that Mary was perpetually a virgin, but this concept could not be substantiated.

2 Jesus accompanied Joseph and Mary to Jerusalem when He was 12 years old (Luke 2:41-52). Jesus stayed in the Temple in the presence of the Jewish leaders when the others returned to Nazareth; He thought it natural that He could be found in "His Father's house".

3 John (2:1-11) recounts the miracle of turning water to wine at a wedding feast. Mary forced Jesus into this first public miracle before Jesus was "ready".

4 Matthew 13:53-57 and Mark 6:1-3 name the brothers James, Joseph, Simon and Judas (plus a reference to sisters) at the event in the Nazareth synagogue. Jesus realized that a prophet is without honor in hometown (note that Jesus did no miracles in Nazareth, because the people were predisposed NOT to believe).

5 After hearing about the many miracles Jesus had performed in various places, "even his brothers did not believe in him." (John 7:5)

6 Several times (Matthew 12:46-50; Mark 3:31-34; Luke 8:19-21) Jesus separated Himself from His family, saying that those who believed were His true sisters and brothers.

7 John 7:1-5 Jesus' cynical brothers goaded Him to go to Judea, where supposedly people would see His miracles for what they were, right out in public.

8 As Paul gives a "report" of Jesus' resurrection to followers, he reports the several times that Jesus appeared to His followers (1 Cor 15:3-7) It is uncertain how Paul knew of this. Other than Paul's brief reference ("... and then He appeared to James." v.7), there is no scriptural basis for this appearance; the described "report" is in the heart and mind of the diarist.

9 NOTE: 1 Cor 15 reports that at the Council of Jerusalem, James was named as leader of the church there in Jerusalem; he later stood to defend Paul and Barnabas. It seems that Paul met James there (Galatians 1:19)

Entry 32. Prayer

1 *NOTE: The "song book" used in Hebrew worship (and for those very early gatherings) was the Old Testament book of Psalms. The topics of those psalms span a wide range of emotions, themes, and commemorations. Many of them are attributed to David, who called for new "songs" to be composed to be used in the Temple worship that David was trying to organize, thus known as "the songs of David".*

2 Jesus spoke of the efficacy of prayer while dealing with the withering fig tree. (Matthew 21:18-22 and Mark 11:20-25)

3 Both Matthew (6:5-14) and Luke (11:1-4) discuss prayer and give the pattern of what we call "the Lord's Prayer". Each reported slightly different words.

4 "Be still…" (Psalm 46:10)

5 Jesus told His followers: "Whatever you ask for, believing in Me…" (Matthew 21:22; Mark 11:24). The verse seems so simple, but the "believing" part puts a great responsibility onto the "asking" part.

Entry 33. The Ascension

1 Luke 24:50-53 mentions this event of Jesus' Ascension into heaven, but a fuller recounting is told at the beginning of Acts (1:1-11).

2 "With God, all things are possible." (Matthew 19:26)

3 *The diarist has taken the liberty to conflate the words of the "Great Commission" given to the disciples when Jesus appeared to them in the Galilee (Matthew 28:16-20) with the account of the Ascension in Acts.*

4 *NOTE: All through the gospels, similar events are recorded having occurred at different times in different places. We know that the gospel writers were trying many years later to remember the exact words said at certain times. How difficult it must have been for the followers to accurately remember all the details.*

Entry 34. Choosing Matthias

1 *NOTE: see notes about Judas in entry 14.*

2 One of the first actions after witnessing the Ascension of Jesus into heaven was to choose a replacement for Judas. (Acts 1:12-26)

3 This prophecy comes from Psalm 109:8.

4 Luke (10:1-23) told of this experience of seventy followers whom Jesus challenged to go out to heal and preach. They were most welcomed by Gentiles and other Jews.

5 *NOTE: remember that lots were used to decide who would "win" Jesus' robe at His crucifixion (reread note in entry #22). This way of making*

decisions was much less frequently reported in the New Testament. It is recorded that the disciples prayed before casting lots to select Matthias; this occasion is the only time in the New Testament that God approved of this manner of choosing.

Entry 35. The Day before Pentecost

1 "I am the resurrection…" (John 11:25-26)

2 "Seek first the kingdom of God…" (Mark 6:33)

3 There is no scriptural basis for the difficulties the followers faced as they waited together for whatever Jesus had in mind when He told them to wait for "the Comforter". This diarist imagined their emotions and reactions.

Entry 36. Pentecost experience

1 *NOTE: Hebrew feasts were considered "God's festivals", that is, days to be commemorated very seriously, as strictly as the Sabbath. Leviticus 23:1-3 lays out the seven annual feast days: Feast of Unleavened Bread (1st and last days, also called Passover); Pentecost (fifty days later, sometimes called the Festival of Weeks); Feast of the Trumpet (Rosh Hashana); Day of Atonement (Yom Kipper); and Feast of Tabernacles (1st and 8th days, also called Succoth). Even in ancient days, it was difficult for devout Hebrews to travel in order to follow the obligation to spend these feast days in the Great Temple. Many faithful Jews still flock to spend time in Jerusalem to commemorate these feast days.*

2 Acts 2:1-4 records this event in the place where the followers were staying. Because it happened during the Jewish festival of Pentecost, we call this experience of the Spirit coming into the hearts and lives of Jesus' followers, "Pentecost".

Entry 37. Aftermath of Pentecost

1 Acts 2: 5-47 describes all that happened when the Spirit-filled followers went out into the city of Jerusalem.

2 *NOTE: That first gathering of Jesus' followers spreading the "good news" of Jesus as Messiah, and the subsequent baptizing of those many who responded to the message marks what is now known as the birthday of the "church".*

Entry 38. Scattering

1 Deuteronomy 16:9-16 describes all the feasts and festivals and how they were to be observed.

2 "Be not afraid" is a consistent message since the beginning: (Genesis 26: 24)

3 *NOTE: Cleopas told the story of his meeting Jesus in Entry 15 of this diary.*

4 *NOTE: According to tradition, Thomas spread the gospel to Persia, where he died. Later tradition places him in India, where he was martyred.*

5 *NOTE: Peter began preaching and teaching in the areas of Samaria, outside of Jerusalem. The first entry of the Book of Acts (of the Apostles) centers on Peter's activities. Peter is the first to report believers who were not previously Jewish. He remained active in the early church development in Jerusalem.*

6 "My peace I leave you…" (John 14:27)

7 Shortly after calling James and John, the sons of Zebedee, Jesus called them "the Sons of Thunder" (Mark 3:17). At that time, it was probably not a favored moniker, Jesus noting their hot temperaments… but time and proximity modified their behavior; John especially became a one of Jesus' most intimate followers.

8 *NOTE: according to tradition, John settled with Mary in the Ephesus area of Asia Minor (now Turkey). After a time of exile on the island of Patmos, he returned to Ephesus, where he is buried (his traditional tomb is at the Church of St. John in Ephesus). Mary's presence in that area is traditionally featured in that city's Islamic sites where she is honored as the mother of the recognized prophet, Jesus.*

9 *NOTE: there is no other mention of Matthias after he was chosen to take Judas' place among the disciples. Tradition says that he journeyed to Ethiopia, where he was martyred.*

10 *NOTE: There are MANY "do not fear" passages in the Old Testament; among them: Psalm 46:1,2a; Jeremiah 1:8; Psalm 23:1.*

11 Isaiah was assured by God's promise: Isaiah 41:10

12 In the book of Acts, Jesus' brother, James, emerged as the leader of the church based in Jerusalem. In the later Council of Jerusalem (Acts 15:12-21), a pathway was decreed for Gentiles to become Christians… clearing the way for this new church (dubbed "Christianity") to become a universal religion.

Entry 39. Into my own future

1 From the cross, Jesus did not proclaim "… surely goodness and kindness will follow me all the days of my life" (Psalm 23), but rather Psalm 22:1: "I cry to you, but you do not answer."

2 *NOTE: Mary Magdalene was indeed a valuable and trusted follower. She was named (Luke 8:2-3) as the woman from whom Jesus cast out seven demons and who then continued to be among the women who followed Jesus and "were helping to support them out of their own means." She*

has long been incorrectly identified as a "woman of ill repute" and as the woman Jesus saved from stoning due to adultery, most possibly since her hometown of Magdala had a reputation for prostitution; the "connection" of Mary Magdalene with these other women is the proximity of written accounts in the scriptures. There is no scriptural evidence of what Mary Magdalene did after leaving Jerusalem (it is the wish of this diarist that she would make a difference in the lives of women in her home town).

[3] *NOTE: Capernaum was located on the north-western end of the Sea of Galilee. It was situated on the major trade route between the East and Jerusalem. It was large enough and important enough that a Roman army unit was garrisoned there to supervise all trade. It was the Romans who assisted in the construction of the large synagogue in Capernaum... and in return, had a (hated) tax collection office attached to that synagogue. Perhaps it was the fear of the Roman presence in Capernaum that resulted in the minimal response to Jesus' teaching.*

[4] After rejection in Nazareth, Capernaum became center of Jesus' ministry. The lack of response to Jesus' message caused Him to curse the city. (Matthew 11:23-24).

[5] *NOTE: The image of a dove has long been seen as a symbol of God's voice. "The Spirit of God descended like a dove" (Matthew 3:16-17; Mark 1:10: Luke 3:21-22) over Jesus' head when He was baptized. John (1:32-34) says that John the Baptist recognized Jesus as the perfect "Lamb of God" when seeing the Spirit descend in the form of a dove after John baptized Jesus in the Jordan River.*

Entry 40. A place in Capernaum

[1] *NOTE: There is little scriptural basis for the other destinations of the many original followers of Jesus. However, tradition has told many stories; some of them tell multiple and different ways that those apostles carried out their callings (those "tugs on their hearts"). Remember that the word "apostle" indicates a follower who is specifically sent, rather than a "disciple" who is still a learner.*

~~THE END~~
At every end, there is
a whole new beginning.

RESOURCES

Holy Bible (New International Version from Zondervan Publishing House). This version includes many explanatory notes, is cross-referenced, and contains a concordance and maps. This is the version the author uses most frequently.

A *concordance* is a list of key words and gives the book, chapter and verse, where they appear in scripture. Many Bibles contain an abbreviated concordance at the back. Serious students might consult *Strong's Exhaustive Concordance* to find every single word (including "and" and "the") in scripture listed in the order in which they appear (James Strong, Abingdon Press, first published in 1890)

Jesus and His Times (a Reader's Digest publication, 1987) This informative volume documents the historical background of Jesus and the key events of His life. It was prepared with the help of leading Biblical scholars and is fully illustrated with paintings of the people and their culture, photographs of the ancient lands today, and maps. Lots of vital information of the world in Jesus' times.

Nelson's Illustrated Bible Dictionary (Guideposts 1986) is an authoritative reference work on the Bible with full-color illustrations.

Author's Note: *Many of the details and notes included in this diary are the result of study and personal travel in Israel and Palestine. Many of the questions raised have been "tackled" (although not necessarily "answered") during thirty years of ministry.*

·

Made in United States
North Haven, CT
14 February 2024